A History of Keighley

HOLY RUSSIA
TO THE BRAVE SONS OF
GREETING AND THANKS FROM THE
BY WORTH
BOROUGH OF KEIGHLEY

A History of Keighley

IAN DEWHIRST

TEMPUS

Frontispiece: The Keighley coat of arms, here carved on a sycamore panel with an additional inscription: 'To the Brave Sons of Holy Russia'. This plaque was sent out to hang above a Keighley bed in an Anglo-Russian Hospital in Petrograd in 1916.

First published 1974
This (revised) edition 2006

Tempus Publishing Limited
The Mill, Brimscombe Port,
Stroud, Gloucestershire, GL5 2QG
www.tempus-publishing.com

British Library Cataloguing in Publication Data.
A catalogue record for this book is available from the British Library.

ISBN 0 7524 3857 3

Typesetting and origination by Tempus Publishing Limited.
Printed in Great Britain.

Contents

List of Illustrations

The illustrations on pages 140 and 143 are reproduced by courtesy of the *Keighley News*; that on page 142 by J.S. Cardwell. The remainder are from items at Keighley Public Library, with the exception of pages 18, 28, 30, 47, 85, 94, 102, 104, 108, 111, 120, 133 and 136, which are from the author's collection.

Keighley Parish Church in the early 1900s.

Introduction

As regards history books, Keighley has fared neither better nor worse than most towns not directly shaping national events. In 1858 one Robert Holmes edited 'the matured results of much diligent inquiry and research' conducted by a late appropriately named William Keighley, into a 211-page volume ponderously entitled *Keighley, Past and. Present; or, an Historical, Topographical, and Statistical Sketch of the Town, Parish, and Environs of Keighley, including Riddlesden, Marley, Hainworth, and some other Places in the Contiguous Parish of Bingley*. This proved sufficiently popular to warrant a revised and enlarged edition in 1879, the year that old John Hodgson, after three years 'collecting materials' to take his mind off his wife's death, brought out his *Textile Manufacture, and Other Industries, in Keighley*. Both demonstrate the period strengths and weaknesses of enthusiastic amateurs with no pretensions to scholarship, in that they threw their facts together in a quaintly haphazard style, but (especially Hodgson) included now illuminating details that a purer historian might well have missed out.

The subsequent century has produced an impressive literature of local churches, chapels, co-operative societies, notabilities, firms, transport systems, public amenities, ranging from the substantial to the extremely slender; but no further general history. The prolific output of dedicated local historians like Fred Williams, Dr Francis Villy and Clifford Whone remains sprinkled through the files of newspapers and journals. In, therefore, attempting to fill something of the deficiency, I have concerned myself chiefly with the last 200 years, for three reasons: *Keighley, Past and Present* remains broadly adequate for the more remote past; there seems little of moment to add to the 'unusually scanty' sources experienced by the town's earlier chroniclers; whilst Keighley's development effectively begins only with the Industrial Revolution. I have, of necessity and with gratitude, relied heavily on many – sometimes anonymous – compilers of local publications, the slender as well as the substantial, as listed in the bibliography of printed sources (which also includes a number of typescript but indispensable items) to be found in the Local Collections of Keighley Central Library and Cliffe Castle Art Gallery and Museum.

My primary aim has been, not the solid accumulation of fact and statistic which can ultimately defeat any but the most determined reader, but rather to present main trends against a more detailed background of their times. In this I have also made extensive use of some hundreds of manuscripts and ephemera in the shape of letters, diaries, accounts, minutes, deeds, pamphlets, broadsheets, programmes, posters ... these are not included in the bibliography, though some are identifiable from the text, and many remain in private hands. The historical value of such sources, often unprepossessing in appearance and easily destroyed, cannot be too strongly emphasised, nor their donation to libraries and archives too unashamedly canvassed. In all cases I have retained exactly the individualistic spelling, grammar and punctuation wherein so much of their flavour lies.

This volume represents one of the means by which the Keighley Town Council is commemorating the demise of the Borough under the local government reorganisation effective from April, 1974. I am therefore deeply indebted to the Keighley Town Council for providing the idea, the opportunity, the financial wherewithal and, above everything else, the working time in which to undertake what has proved an enjoyable but spectacularly time-consuming venture. My thanks are also due to Mr Fred Taylor, F.L.A., Chief Librarian, and the staff of the Reference Department at Keighley Central Library, for their long forbearance during a period when my attention to the daily round has not, of necessity, been entirely whole-hearted. So many individuals have helped me by their loan or gifts of material, that I must confine myself to naming but a few: unique items came from Mrs V. Fattorini, Mrs E.L. Fletcher. Dr J. Prentice, and Messrs E. Binns, S.R. Boardman, G.E.S. Dunlop. T.P. Maude, J. Ogden and W. Place. Naturally, any errors or misinterpretations are my own.

Ian Dewhirst
Keighley, September 1973

Chapter One

Domesday Book – prehistoric times – Roman roads – spelling changes – Market Charter – Flodden Field – parish registers – Civil War – the Revd Oliver Heywood – the Revd Miles Gale's History of the Free School in Kighley – eighteenth-century development – Turnpike Trusts – Leeds & Liverpool Canal – Low Mill

Cyhha, an Old English thane passed otherwise into oblivion, had cultivated a forest clearing and given his name to what we now call Keighley. This the Norman clerks found, compiling William the Conqueror's Domesday Book in 1086: 'In Chichelai, Ulchel, and Thole, and Ravensuar, and William had six carucates to be taxed'.

We are indebted to those Normans for our first written record of the district. The Saxon landscape they surveyed emerges sketchily, its heavily wooded valleys dotted with clearings (-ley and -thwaite place-names), its higher ground with enclosures (-worth place-names). Land was measured by the carucate, traditionally the extent that could be cultivated with one plough and eight oxen in one year – upwards of 120 acres, by a probably generous local estimate. In Utley (Utta's clearing), one William was taxed on a carucate; William and Gamelbar shared another at Oakworth (oak-tree enclosure). William held a carucate at Newsholme (new houses); Ravensuar, two at Laycock (small stream); Ardulf, one at Riddlesden (Rethel's valley) – probably that same Ardulf who, with four carucates at Morton (moorland farmstead), ranked as the locality's biggest landowner; whilst Ernegis had one at Marley (a clearing frequented by martens) and a half at Hainworth (Hagena's enclosure), 'and they are waste', having presumably suffered during the Conqueror's subjection of the North.

Preceding millennia had left tantalising fragments of those who had peopled the higher ground above swampy prehistoric valleys. Mesolithic flint workers bequeathed a scattering of tools and weapons across Harden and Haworth and Oakworth Moors; at Shepherd's Hill, on the ridge of Rombalds Moor, they had made scrapers and knives. Rombalds Moor, especially, commemorates their Bronze Age successors in the shape of stone circles, burial mounds, and the religious symbolism of their cup and ring stones. Iron Age man had built earthworks on Cullingworth and Addingham Moors.

The Romans came and went in their turn, leaving little save the conjectural route of their Manchester to Ilkley road, crossing Airedale between Hainworth Shaw and West Morton, and bisected by another road following the present Hollins Lane towards Elslack. They also presented later generations with a mystery. Some time before the middle of the third century, Romans buried, for reasons unknown, a copper chest full of coins near their Manchester-Ilkley road, where farmer Simon Mitchell dug it up at Elam Grange in 1775. The denarii – according to the erudite Dr Whitaker – included 'every Emperor from Nero to Pupienus, Pertinax and Didius Julianus only excepted'; and they weighed 100lbs. In a wild, spectacular scramble for pickings (antiquarians were paying from eightpence to ten shillings per coin), the local Georgian population dispersed the treasure as effectively as if it had been buried afresh!

'Chichelai' of the Domesday Book would undergo, through centuries of Charters and Assize Rolls, a multitude of forms: Kichalaie, Kychelay, Kykelei, Kyhele, Kyhhelay, Kikhele, Kygheley, Kithelai, Kygeley, Keghelay – not till the mid-sixteenth century did the spelling 'Keighley' emerge, and this would continue interchangeable with 'Kighley' till the early nineteenth century.

Our few recorded events suggest a developing Medieval community. Keighley's first parish church was founded in the twelfth century. In 1305, Edward I granted a Market Charter to Henry de Keighley, whose family were lords of the manor for sixteen generations: markets were held every Wednesday, with a fair 'on the eve on the day and on the day following of St Simon and St Jude' which would survive, early each November, into the 1920s. The Poll Tax returns of 1379 listed forty-seven couples and fifteen single people in Keighley – at the same time, Haworth was credited with sixty-four inhabitants, Steeton fifty-eight, Skipton one hundred and twenty-seven.

1513 saw a scratch English army hurrying north to defeat the invading James IV of Scotland at the battle of Flodden Field, in Northumberland. To a Craven contingent led by Lord Clifford, Keighley contributed forty-seven soldiers – twenty-nine bowmen, sixteen billmen and two mounted bowmen – some of whose names (Brigg, Butterfield, Clough, Sugden, Stell) would recur in the later history of the locality.

The Parish Registers of St Andrew's Church, begun in 1562, hint at the early existence of a modest woollen industry: two clothiers, John Hartley and John Blakey, were buried in 1571. From the Parish Registers, too, peep occasional human characters:

November, 1572. 'The xxiiijth daie Agnes Broughton alias faire Agnes was buried'.
December, 1623. 'Richard the son of John Sugden alias Loynend was buried the ijth day'.
March, 1647. 'Auld Nell buried the 26th daye'.

Of the plagues which ravaged Europe for centuries, Keighley retains its share of undated traditions, like the chilling oral reminiscence of 'a time when so many died of a pestilence at Morton Banks that people lay unburied in their homes and cattle died untended in their byres'. One definite record survives, in the Parish

Registers for October, 1645 (a bad plague year for the West Riding), when disease claimed, within a fortnight, John Watters 'of Pinfould' and three of his children, Jane and Martha Sutcliffe, Joseph Brigg and two children, and 'the wife of Chr. Sugden'.

A Parliamentary garrison during the Civil War possibly accounts for the name Guard House. Twelve soldiers were buried between 1643 and 1645; two 'slayne at new brigge' and four buried together suggest skirmishes; whilst tradition speaks of a raid by 150 Royalist troopers from Skipton in February of 1645, in the course of which Major John Hughes, Lieutenant-Governor of Skipton Castle and 'a most valiant souldier', was mortally wounded.

The small seventeenth-century town, clustered about its Parish Church, remains scantily documented. 'The Aire, having passed Craven, is carried in a much larger channel, with pleasant fields on both sides, by Kighley,' William Camden tersely relates in his *Britannia* of 1586 – being preoccupied, after the fashion of early topographers, with the local gentry in the shape of the Keighley family and their Market Charter. A rhymster known variously as Barnaby Harrington or 'Drunken Barnaby', publishing his *Travels to the North* about the mid-1600s, is slightly more informative:

Thence to Kighley, where are mountains
Steepy threat'ning, living fountains;
Rising hills, and barren vallies,
Yet bon socios and good fellows;
Jovial, jocund, jolly bowlers,
As they were the world's controllers.

The Revd Oliver Heywood, peripatetic Nonconformist preacher and diarist, visited Keighley quite often, and chronicled the deaths of Henry Smith whilst 'drinking with some gentlemen at Jo. Learoyds on Wednesday night, Nov. 15. 1682' ('ranting, singing, shouting, leaned forward, froth coming out of his mouth, immediatly dyed, drunk'), and of a Kildwick man walking home from Keighley Fair two years later, 'found dead leaning upon a gate'. Heywood had cause, indeed, to remember Keighley: his son was persuaded to drink over-freely there ('he not fit to goe out, fell off his horse'); and his prayer-meeting in 1672 was interrupted by 'one West', supposedly a Quaker who had 'marryed two wives at one time'. Keighley was, according to the Revd Oliver Heywood, 'a barren place for religion'!

The town's first known historian arrived in the quaint, cantankerous character of the Revd Miles Gale, Rector from 1680 to 1720, a dilettante artist, antiquarian, mathematician, geologist and, curiously, manufacturer of 'a Hexapode, of six different pieces, fastened without glue or nails, yet not now to be severed, with the best turned tobacco-stopper'. Happily for local posterity, Gale 'writ an account of the town and parish of Kighley', which was subsequently published in Thomas Gent's *History of Ripon* (1733) and *The Gentleman's Magazine* (1815).

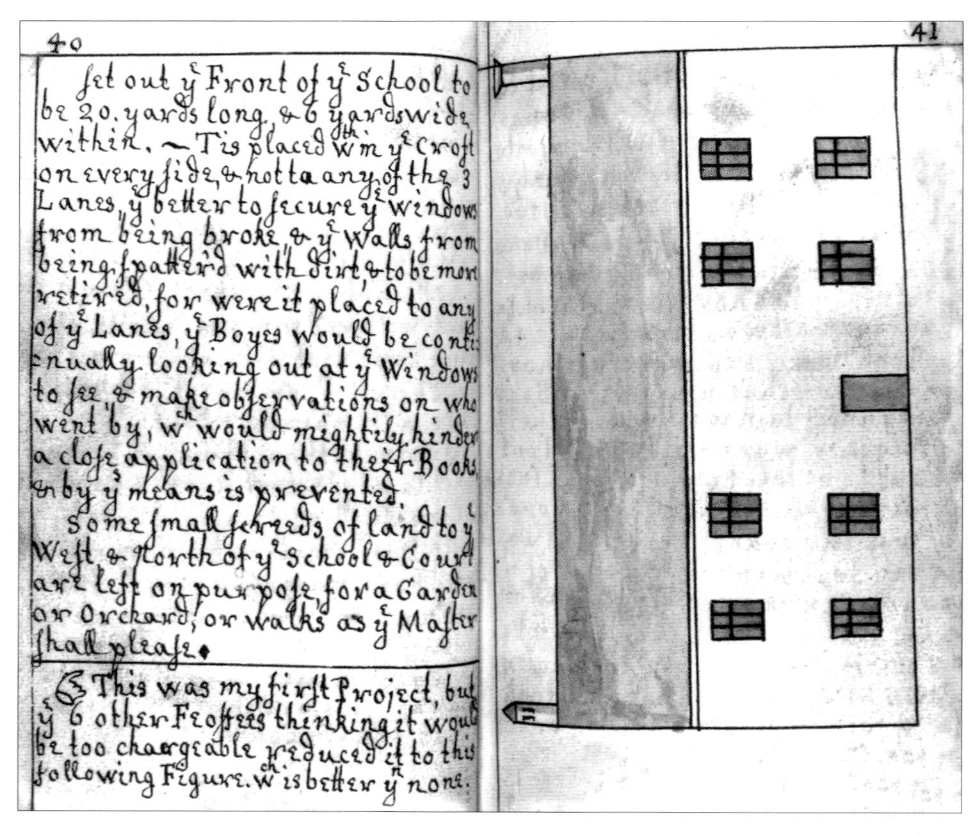

40

set out ye Front of ye School to be 20. yards long, & 6 yards wide within. – 'Tis placed wth in ye Croft on every side, & not to any of the 3 Lanes, ye better to secure ye windows from being broke & ye Walls from being spatter'd with dirt, & to be more retired, for were it placed to any of ye Lanes, ye Boyes would be continually looking out at ye Windows to see, & make observations on who went by, wch would mightily hinder a close application to their Books, & by ys means is prevented.

Some small shreds of land to ye West & North of ye School & Court are left on purpose, for a Garden or Orchard, or walks as ye Master shall please.

This was my first Project, but ye 6 other Feoffees thinking it would be too chargeable reduced it to this following Figure. wch is better yn none.

41

Two pages from the Revd Miles Gale's History of the Free School in Kighley*, showing his drawing of the building.*

Keighley's inhabitants, it transpired, had been counted in 1695, when 'there appeared to be in this parish 1,704', whose one hundred houses were 'pleasantly situated in a low valley, surrounded with hills' – from Hainworth (presumably on a clear day) the Rector had viewed Pendle Hill, Penyghent and Ingleborough. He noted the town's position at 'the meeting of two brooks' (the River Worth and the North Beck, one already having a mill on its banks) near a single-arched stone bridge which, characteristically, he had measured: 'from the basis to the crown of the battlement, is nine yards, and wide at the foot 22 yards'. A mile away, the River Aire seethed, almost, with dace, grayling, minnows, perch. eels, gudgeons, trout, smelts, and salmon which 'poor people' would catch at Michaelmas 'with blazing and iron forks'. Otters abounded, 'which we suppose to feed on muscles, because the shells are generally found empty'.

Water from a spring 'a mile to the West' above the town – possibly Jennet's Well at Black Hill – was conveyed by stone troughs through 'the chief street' for the convenience of householders. The Parish Church had been equipped with new pews in 1703, and 'made uniform as to the windows' seven years later. A tablet 'set up in the middle quire of the church, over the vestry', recorded the benefactions which – in conjunction with the poor rate – maintained paupers, who were numerous.

'A traveller through this parish,' Gale announced, 'shall not meet with half a mile of level ground', save 'a field of plain earth' to the east, where horse-races were run – probably the present Victoria Park area, the scene of sundry rumbustious activities till the nineteenth century. 'I have seen an old horse run with ten men at certain distances,' observed the worthy Rector, 'delivering of a handkerchief one to another; when the horse lost. At another time a horse with twenty men, when the men lost. At another time, a galloway being matched with a large horse to run this course round ten times, without heats, the owner of the horse not daring to run, the galloway ran by itself, which was fifteen miles, the course once round being a mile and a half'.

In 1716 the corner-stones of a Grammar School were laid in Cook Lane. Innkeeper John Drake had noticed Keighley's educational paucity — 'whereby,' according to Miles Gale, 'for want of knowledge some were seduced by that vile sect of the Quakers, and others by that wicked crew of the Anabaptists, to follow false ways of worship' and, as his epitaph jauntily informs:

Houses and Land he left to be
A Free-School Master's salary.
He lived and died without a mate,
And yielded to the laws of fate.

Drake had envisaged a respectable bachelor schoolmaster teaching Latin and Greek at a salary of £25 a year; which, together with a further endowment from Jonas Tonson a few years later, formed the basis for Keighley's considerable educational achievement.

The Revd Miles Gale's *History of the Free Grammar School in Kighley* has never been published; indeed, the Victorian author of *Keighley, Past and Present* could not believe that 'this singular MS' was ever meant for public scrutiny, 'it being freely interlarded with strong invective and personal abuse, more calculated to injure than promote good morals'. From the number of handwritten and typed copies, however, it has obviously supplied 'underground' reading in the town for the past two and a half centuries. If Gale's untidy potpourri of narrative, correspondence, sermons, verses and drawings details (against a background of ale-house tipplings) his quarrels with the rest of John Drake's trustees, it also presents a more engaging aspect of his (and human) nature. We leave the good Rector with one further quotation:

> On Thursday, Dec. 24. 1713, being ye last day ye Masons would work before Xmas, I went in ye morning to ye School-Croft, where 5 of ym were at work, being almost at ye end of their stones, having then hewed for 14 2 light transome Windows. I wished ym to finish

> what I intended for ye ground work at yt time, but they answered yt two Feoffees [trustees] had been with ym ye day before & discharged ym from digging any further. Upon my urging it a 2nd time they replyed if I would come again after dinner they would digg out ye 2 sides to my proposed length (wch was 20 yards) but would not cross ye southend, willing for to have so much of ye work done, I promissd to come, in ye afternoon & staying half an hour longer for a peice of bodily exercise, I took a Spade & graved up ye sodds on ye East-side to its just length there having been 17 yards before. I would yn have proceeded to digg more deep, but it proving stoney, & being in a great Coat, & beginning to sweat & be weary wth so hard work, thought good to desist. In ye afternoon about 3 I went again in hopes to have carried on ye work so farr as in ye morning we had discoursed on, but ye Masons were all fled, as I supposed out of fear to disoblige some of ye Feoffees, but they pretended it was to heat their Ovens For Pies agst Xmass.

The eighteenth century witnessed a steady development. Keighley's estimated population had topped 2,000 by 1730, 3,000 by 1755, 4,000 by 1780. A cottage woollen and worsted industry existed: one Joseph Craven, of Laycock, sent shalloon pieces (a light fabric used for linings) to London early in the century; whilst the Parish Registers include the occupations of fulling miller, yarn dealer, comb-maker, shalloon maker, and – repeatedly by the 1730s – woolcomber, and serge, linen tape and garter weaver. If yeoman and husbandman as yet remained prominent, agriculture was in process of expansion at the expense of common lands. An Act of Parliament for the enclosure of Oxenhope Moor was obtained in 1771; another, covering 'open fields, arable lands, meadows, commons and waste' at Keighley, Thwaites and Newsholme, in 1780; a third for 'common or waste called Morton Moor or Rumbles Moor' in 1788.

The age, too, saw better communications, thanks largely to the Turnpike Trusts, bodies usually of landowners who undertook to repair, maintain, and in some instances improve roads, in exchange for the levying of tolls. From Keighley to Hebden Bridge would remain a formidable track — by Oxenhope, the Top of the Stairs and Crimsworth Dean — till 1814 and the building of the Cockhill Moor road; to Colne, a no less bleak weathering of Two Laws and the Herders; to Halifax, a laboured climb up Park Lane and Hainworth Shaw to Cullingworth — though the Ingrow and Cross Roads route would be made in 1794. But if the traditional ways to Bradford went via Park Lane and Harden, or Marley, Beckfoot and Cottingley, there was also, by 1754 when Stockbridge was widened, a 'great and common high road leading between Lancashire and Yorkshire' following much the same course as the modern Keighley to Bradford route. Again, the Keighley and Kendal Turnpike Trust was formed in 1753, responsible for a road that wound towards Skipton by way of Cook Lane, Spring Gardens, Hollins Lane and Steeton Bank. In 1782, the opening of Old Bar House Lane from Green Head brought the route down to its present course below Hawkcliffe Wood, whilst North Street was laid out in 1786; though it would be 1825 before the building of the section from Keighley through Utley to Hawkcliffe.

A N

A C T

F O R

Dividing and Incloſing the Common and Waſte Grounds within the Village, Hamlet, Townſhip, and Manor of *Oxenhope*, in the Pariſh of *Bradford* and County of *York*.

HEREAS there is a large common Moor or Tract of waſte Ground called *Oxenhope Moor*, lying and being in the Village, Hamlet, Townſhip, and Manor of *Oxenhope*, in the Pariſh of *Bradford* and Weſt Riding of the County of *York*, containing by Eſtimation Two thouſand Five hundred Acres or thereabouts : — **Preamble.**

And whereas Dame *Eleanor Aſheton*, Sir *Thomas Egerton*, Baronet, *Samuel Egerton*, Eſquire, *Charles Wood*, and *Abraham Balme*, Gentlemen, are Lady and Lords of the ſaid Manor, and they and *Benjamin Ferrand*, Eſquire, *Richard Greenwood*, *George Greenwood*, *William Greenwood*, *John Roberts*, *Joſeph Ruſhworth*, *John Murgetroyd*, and the Reverend *John Richardſon*, Clerk, and ſeveral other Perſons and their Truſtees,

A — Leſſees,

The opening of the 'Act for Dividing and Inclosing' Oxenhope Moor, 1771.

A relic of the turnpikes, this Stockbridge toll-house was demolished in 1972.

Keighley's position on the Aire Gap ensured its proximity to the Leeds and Liverpool Canal, begun in 1770 and not completed until 1816. The Bingley to Skipton stretch, however, was opened in 1773, when the first two boat-loads of coal were sold at half-price in honour of the occasion, church bells were rung, and 'there were also bonfires, illuminations, and other demonstrations of joy' – emigration advertisements were shortly offering an idyllic passage by canal from Bingley to 'Skipton, Liverpool, and America'!

But Keighley's possibly most important date was June 30th, 1780. That was the day the new Low Mill began spinning cotton. It was the first cotton mill in Yorkshire, and its owners, two Lancashire men called Clayton and Walshman, had to send their child workers to Sir Richard Arkwright's factory at Cromford in Derbyshire, to learn the processes. The Industrial Revolution had arrived in Keighley.

Chapter Two

Dr Whitaker – cotton and worsted industries – a proposed branch canal – masters and workers – factory conditions –the Sadler Committee

Thomas Dunham Whitaker, Vicar of Whalley, published his *History and Antiquities of the Deanery of Craven* in 1805. Epitomising the cultured eighteenth-century gentleman-historian, he waxed eloquent over the beauties and departed glories of Skipton and Barden and Bolton Abbey; Keighley, however, was a different matter: 'This parish lies immediately North from that of Bingley, in the course of the Are, with little which can interest the eye, the memory, or the imagination. I may therefore be excused if I betray some anxiety to reach more pleasing scenes; for hard is the fate of a Topographer while he respires the smoke of manufactories and is stunned by the din of recent population'.

Dr Whitaker's 'recent population' had numbered 5,745 at the first census in 1801 – one-third again more than the estimated 4,100 of 1780 – and he had scant respect for the 'manufactories' responsible for their increase: 'Before the introduction of manufactories, the parish of Kighley did not want [lack] its retired glens and well-wooded hills; but the clear mountain torrent now is defiled, its scaly inhabitants suffocated by filth, its murmurs lost in the din of machinery, and the native music of its overhanging groves exchanged for oaths and curses'.

Behind that faultless diction and unashamed nostalgia lies a sober realism. No more would the euphemistic 'scaly inhabitants' of the Aire and the Worth and the North Beck swim in a 'clear mountain torrent': Dr Whitaker was witnessing the beginnings of an inevitable spoliation which would destroy the perch and grayling, the salmon, eels and otters of Miles Gale's local landscape. The last two decades of the eighteenth and the opening of the nineteenth century saw a proliferation of mills, powered by water and spinning cotton. Though, within a few years, steam-turned machinery would develop, and the application of roller-spinning also to wool would shift the locality's industrial emphasis to worsted, it should never be forgotten that Keighley's growth was founded on cotton, whilst the waters of the River Worth and the North Beck provided the motive power.

The North (or, as it was then, the Laycock) Beck became no longer rural, its course traced by factories: Newsholme Higher and Lower Mills, Goose Eye, Wood Mill, Holme House and Holme Mill, Castle Mill, North Brook Mill. ... Along, or connected to, the Worth came Dalton Mill, Low Mill, Walk Mill, East and West Greengate, Grove Mill, Damems Mill. ... Farther out of town they sprang up, at Ponden and Spring Head and Higher Providence. ... Sandywood Mill utilised streams running down the present Highfield and Spring Gardens Lanes. ... Only Low Bridge, Damside and Hope Mills, of all Keighley's cotton factories, did not rely on water-power; they were worked by 'crank motion', a forerunner of Watt's steam engine.

The men responsible for those early mills enjoyed initiative in common, but the adjuncts of ability, means and luck were less evenly distributed, and competition ran keen. Low Mill built a tail goit which would have cut off Dalton Mill's water supply, but a lawsuit prevented their using it. John Hodgson, among the chatty reminiscences of his *Textile Manufacture, and other Industries, in Keighley*, has a tale about John Greenwood of North Brook Mill, which speaks volumes:

> At first Mr Greenwood was seriously put about by a defect in his spinning operation, for which he could not find a remedy; one day, however, he saw a girl going past his mill who worked at the Low Mill, he was acquainted with the girl, and knew that she was employed at the Low Mill, when he saw her he accosted her in the most friendly manner, saying, 'Betty, I have begun cotton spinning,' when she answered, 'Yes, I understand you have,' he then said, 'Will you step in and look at us,' she did so, when he told her that he could not make the bobbins draw, and that the yarn formed what is called a snarle on the top of the flyer; she at once examined the spindle, and lifting up the bobbin she exclaimed, 'You have no washer.' 'Washer,' said he, 'what's a washer,' when she said, 'If you will let me have a bit of cloth and a pen knife I will make you one.' He at once pulled out his pen knife and cut a piece of cloth out of his coat lap, from which she shaped a washer, and, having placed it under the bobbin, it drew to perfection, when he put his hand into his pocket and gave her half a guinea...

Not surprisingly, the Greenwood family emerged pre-eminent among Keighley's first industrialists, with interests in North Brook, West Greengate, Cabbage and Screw Mills, Vale Mill at Oakworth, and Swarcliffe Mill, near Ripon.

Others – and not all were men: one Betty Hudson built Damside Mill; whilst Dalton Mill (named after its manager) was started by Rebecca Leach of West Riddlesden Hall, described by one of her workers as 'a bold and masculine sort of woman' – fared less well. James Fox, builder of Low Bridge Mill, failed, as did his successor John Ellison. Castle Mill ruined William Wilkinson, his son bankrupted, with many more, in the financial collapse of the Butterworth Panic of 1826. The Ropers went from comparative riches to rags at Damems Mill. At Damside Mill by 1806, Thomas Parker was in debt to the tune of £1,380 16s – John Greenwood was one of his creditors. Thomas Corlass of Hope Mill 'one morning went to the

Letterhead engravings of Keighley mills: the Walk Mill …

… and, at a slightly later and more sophisticated stage, Grove Mill.

engine tenter and ordered him to rake out the fire and stop the engine; and this being done, he from that time ceased to be a cotton spinner'.

The Industrial Revolution – notoriously – relied heavily on the labour of women and children. The Greenwoods had an arrangement for employing young orphan girls from the Foundling Hospital, London; and an early if modest piece of factory legislation was enshrined in an Act of 1802 requiring 'Overseers and Guardians of the Poor, to keep a Register of the several Children who shall be bound or assigned by them as Apprentices'. One such Keighley Register includes several cotton spinners amongst those to whom pauper children were bound: Thomas Corlass was assigned twelve-year-old Samuel Abbott, John Shackleton a fourteen-year-old Susan Waddington; John Roper and Joseph Greenwood took on boys aged nine.

A lifetime later, one of the first local child workers, as yet unprotected by legislation, would pen a brief unpunctuated autobiography. His name was John Kitson, and he had been born in 1781 at Belle Isle, near Haworth, and his father had gone for a soldier 'when I was but a child so as I could not tell on him going', leaving his mother with 'three lads Joseph Joshua and me'.

> ... I went to the free school for some were near one year and when I was about five years of age I Began spinning worstied yarn and had five hanks set for my work a day from thence we went to live at Haworth Hall I span there till I was about seven years of age and I had seven Hanks for my work But there was one called Blakey that took a mill at Bridgehouse of Mr Greenwoods and span cotton and I Began to go there when I was about seven years of age and tented five pair of cards near three years ... then I Left there and went to a mill called Whright mill there I went to work near three years in the night then they took me out to make up twist and I did that near two years ...

At the age of fifteen he was a veteran workman, and had lamed himself. His reminiscences are without rancour, plain matter-of-fact. 'That,' he is simply stating, 'is how life was'. As an old man in his seventies, in the 1850s, he fretted because he was out of work.

John Kitson, it will be noted, was 'spinning worstied yarn' when he was five. Though this, in 1786, refers to a cottage industry, mechanised worsted spinning lagged behind cotton by only a few years. In the Keighley district by the beginning of the nineteenth century, cotton mills were gradually being converted to worsted. By the time Edward Baines published his *History, Directory and Gazetteer of the County of York* in 1823, Keighley listed only four cotton spinners and manufacturers, as opposed to 44 worsted manufacturers. The former, inevitably, included John Greenwood & Sons; whilst, among the latter, some notable names were emerging: Calvert and Clapham; Craven and Briggs; John Hanson; Richard Hattersley & Sons; B. & W. Marriner; Jonas Sugden; John & William Haggas; Isaac Butterfield. ... Fourteen years later, William White's West Riding Directory was crediting Keighley with five cotton and no less than sixty worsted manufacturers.

The era, albeit unquestionably one of industrial development on a spectacular scale, was inherent with problems. There was the matter of transport. That roads were proving inadequate for increased traffic, whilst the Leeds and Liverpool Canal was being insufficiently exploited locally, is suggested by proposals of 1819 to build a branch canal into Keighley. The trouble with the Leeds and Liverpool Canal was the mile separating the town from its nearest wharves at Stockbridge. So, on January 12th 1819, a number of 'the principal gentlemen, tradesmen, manufacturers, and inhabitants' met at the Devonshire Arms Inn and unanimously agreed that plans should be prepared for 'a Branch Canal to Keighley from the Leeds and Liverpool Canal'. Resulting enquiries disclosed that an estimated 400 loads of coals per day were being carted into the neighbourhood. Manufacturers were responsible for more than twenty tons of goods going to and from Bradford by road every week, which, it was opined, 'could be conveyed by the canal in a Fly or market Boat'.

The branch canal was envisaged as leading from Utley, crossed by eleven road and occupation bridges and bordered with a flagged 'track path or hawling Road', into a central Keighley basin complete with wharves and warehouses. The scheme came to nothing – it would have cost an estimated £31,455 – though it is fascinating to imagine the difference it would have made to the landscape north of the town: 'To pass the River Aire at or near Uttley, it will be necessary to build an Aqueduct of Twelve Arches over the River, besides Two smaller ones for roadways…'

The age had other, and deeper, problems. The 1811 census showed a Keighley of 6,864 inhabitants. In 1821, this had swung to 9,223; by 1831, 11,176; 1841, 13,378; and 1851, 18,258. A population, doubling in thirty years and trebling in fifty, had lost the comparative stability of earlier generations. Against a background, nationally, of the Napoleonic Wars, unemployment, corn riots and machine-breaking, new concepts of mechanisation, of mass production, and of the relationship between masters and workers, were being untidily thrashed out.

In November of 1812, their tempers doubtless exacerbated by recent West Riding Luddite disturbances, some thirty Keighley worsted manufacturers meeting at the Devonshire Arms considered 'the Articles entered into by a Society of Woolcombers, calling themselves "The United Societies of Great-Britain"' to be 'unjust and pernicious to both Master and Workman'. Their resolutions were published as handbills:

> That we, the undersigned, will not on any Account or Pretence whatever, after the Twenty-third Day of November, Instant, employ, or suffer to be employed, any Workman who is now and shall continue to be, or who hereafter may be connected with any Society or Societies of a similar Nature.

Again, in 1825 during the 23-week strike of the Bradford Union Association of Woolcombers and Stuff Weavers, a majority of Keighley manufacturers, chaired by William Sugden of Eastwood House, resolved:

> 1st. That it is our determination to turn all off who are in the Combers and Weavers Union.
>
> 2nd. That it is our determination to turn all off who can be ascertained to support the Combers and Weavers Union in any manner either direct or indirect.

The infant trade unions, which so aroused manufacturers' ire, had developed largely from sick clubs. The New Union Friendly Society, for example, meeting at the Sun Inn, Haworth, had been formed in 1781 for the purpose of 'aiding and assisting the Members thereof, in Sickness, and Infirmities'. By 1787 Keighley boasted a pleasantly-named Affectionate Society, its transactions shakily recorded in a most laborious minute-book: 'March 5th. a Greed by the comitey and Isack Sugden on a count of a Lamenes on is right ne that He Shal not rec.v No Benifit from this Sociaty on a count of that Lamenes as witnas our Hands' – of the thirteen signatories, five, illiterate, made their marks.

Between 1799 and 1824 the Combination Acts prohibited workers' unions as contrary to the public interest. Yet friendly societies flourished, like the Royal Union Benefit Society founded at Keighley in 1811 and 'holden at the house of Betty Fox, Innkeeper' (public houses provided the customary venue, their perquisites being the dinners and quarts of ale supplied at meetings and funerals). Describing themselves as 'a Society of Workmen and other Persons, being free and accepted Masons', members set about 'raising a Stock or Fund of Money, for the mutual Aid and Assistance of each other, labouring under any of the Calamities or Afflictions with which a wise and good Providence might see fit to visit them in this transitory Life'. The subscription was 10s 6d per quarter. When ill – provided disability was 'not occasioned by immoral conduct' – members drew 6s a week; if they died, their next of kin got two guineas towards funeral expenses.

From friendly society to trade club was a short step. By the 1820s Keighley had three Combers' Clubs, meeting respectively at the Fleece, the Lord Rodney, and the Black Bull Inn, Damside. They were linked with similar organisations throughout Yorkshire and Lancashire, and further afield; since, in addition to acting as sick clubs, they provided hospitality for unemployed members perforce 'tramping for work'. Old John Hodgson recalled an interesting feature: 'When calling at the workshops, or combshops, as they were called, if they did not obtain employment, each club-man was required by the rules of the club to pay the man out of work one half-penny; this may seem a small sum, but during flat times, or on the occurrence of a strike in some neighbouring town, sometimes as many as a dozen or a score would call in one day, which made it a heavy tax upon those who were in work'. Not unnaturally, in times of unrest – as in 1825 when the strike fund of the Bradford combers and weavers was being swelled by contributions from other towns – employers tended to clamp down on their more union-minded workers.

But an industrial history centred on disputes can present an unbalanced, if dramatic, picture. For details of everyday life we are indebted to crumbling copperplate books like one headed, on each page: *An Account of the Time Worked at Vale Mill with anything remarkable that may occur.* At the period, in the 1820s, Vale Mill, tucked into the Worth Valley between Oakworth and Haworth, was spinning cotton and depending largely on water-power. Its goit and dams were vital; time was recorded as gained or lost 'by the Water-Clock'; and repeated though unexplained references to 'getting the planks up' and putting them down again probably relate to a means of regulating the supply. When their upper dam burst, one Sunday in 1820, they necessarily began repairs 'as soon as light' on the Monday morning, finding evidence of Saturday-night vandalism as, among other things, 'the bye fall clow [sluice] was broke and thrown into the Goit'. Work sometimes 'stood for water' in dry weather, though periods of drought were not wholly wasted:

> June 7th, 1824. 'Very hot and Dry. Cleared our Goit of the Stones. Lowered the part next the Grate & Got the Stones over. The Men Laded the Old Damstones bottom for Fish – And then was repaired the footings of the Wall. Also the Wall itself this Day.

Water, or the lack of it, was not the only problem. There was a steam pan which kept breaking, and trouble with cardroom cylinders, and accidents: Hannah Pickles broke her leg – 'both Bones' – and James Judson was 'hurt with the Card'; Betty Hay nipped her finger, while Nancy Rushworth 'nipped two finger ends off and cut her head at the double Picker'. In February of 1822 'our Reelers turned out for more Wage'. This was 'fixed' (whether before or after the strike is not clear) 'at 14 Reels for a Shilling', but two days later the mill was losing speed for want of bobbins, 'the Reelers being off'. The outcome is not recorded, though the foreman 'heard John Wood's Complaints before the Master'. (Wood features again in a somewhat ambiguous accident of 1824: 'The Shaft fell, on John Wood head and broke it, in three places'!). One senses, however, the satisfaction in a later entry, which dismisses weather and circumstances in the same breath: 'Fine day, Pulled off the weavers wage 6d'.

Otherwise, the Vale Mill Time Book reveals little or nothing of that inhumanity which we can now perhaps too glibly imagine of nineteenth-century factories. The foreman and probable keeper of the daily record emerges as a kindly man who, by his death in 1825, had lent a total of £16 18s 9d to twenty-four people. True, Ann Pighills and Betty Brown were turned off 'for bringing Knitting'; but, on the other hand, when the Light Horse rode by in 1821, work stopped so that everybody could go out to watch.

Workers enjoyed only three full days' holiday in a typical year, 1821 — December 25th and 26th, and August 28th. Half-days, however, were sprinkled through the months: the 'Old Christmas' on January 6th; Shrove Tuesday, Easter Monday and Whit Monday; Keighley Fair in May and November, Bingley Tide in August, Haworth Tide in October. In 1821 they got an extra half-day, being 'short of water' — though work lost through water shortages was often made up in the dinner hour.

A harsher indictment of the factory system is the evidence collected in 1832 by a committee formed by Michael Thomas Sadler, Member of Parliament for Aldborough and an exponent of reform. Sir Robert Peel's Factory Act of 1819 had applied only to children working in the cotton industry; and, although specifying a minimum age limit of nine, and a maximum working day of twelve hours for nine to sixteen-year-olds, was not generally enforced. An Act of 1825 introduced the idea of a Saturday part-holiday (only nine hours' work!); another, in 1831, prohibited night-shifts for those under twenty-one. By then, the Ten Hours Movement had gained momentum: hence, the Sadler Committee's investigation of the case for regulating the hours of child labour. It is fair to observe that contemporary objections to the Sadler Committee, on the grounds that its evidence was exaggerated, may not be entirely unjustified; certainly, witnesses were carefully selected, were not under oath, and leading questions were put to them. Nevertheless, their testimony speaks eloquently. Those questioned included five Keighley men.

Abraham Wildman was an earnest, 28-year-old Sunday School teacher who had published a little book of rather indifferent *Miscellaneous Poems* in 1829. One was called 'The Factory Child's Complaint':

Ere the lark salute the skies,
Ere the sun upon us smile,
From our wretched beds we rise,
Weary with the last day's toil.

Summoned by yon hateful bell
Morn and noon we're doomed to hear,
Yes, it sounds like death's dull knell,
We its victims of despair'.

Wildman would become secretary of a local Short-Time Committee, would send a petition to the Duke of Wellington and be acquainted with Richard Oastler. Now, he told the Sadler Committee about his four sisters working at Castle Mill – 'generally' twelve hours a day, though 'when they had a strong order on hand to finish, they got up in the morning by half past four o'clock', returning home at eleven at night. He felt, too, that factory conditions were detrimental to morals: he knew one mill employing eighteen women, of whom twelve had illegitimate children, 'some as many as three a-piece'; and opined that children should be given 'a little time' for moral and religious instruction – a modest enough demand, under the circumstances. When asked for his impressions of the physical appearance of Keighley children, he replied:

> 'I have observed them in the Sunday-school, and at times in the street, living in the midst of them, that they have not that healthy appearance we see children generally have in the country; frequently without arms, without legs, and without fingers; and we can produce in Keighley 150 rickety, crooked-legged children, owing to their being over-wrought'.

(Again, it should be observed that forty years later a Keighley doctor, who had taught with Wildman in the same Sunday School, would write: 'I can, in all good faith, affirm that I never witnessed anything of the kind'.)

Gillett Sharpe, an assistant Overseer of the Poor questioned about cases of deformity in Keighley, said he 'had an opportunity of visiting other towns, and it is my opinion, according to my observation, that there is not another town worse, in proportion, to the size of it'. Like Wildman, he was concerned about the lack of morals in factories, and he too mentioned the mill with the eighteen women. As overseer, he paid out nearly £50 a month for the support of bastard children — 1s 6d kept a child for a week, and Keighley's population was 'eleven thousand, and some odd'. Presumably the Committee did their own arithmetic.

Like Wildman, Joseph Firth was acquainted with Richard Oastler, and in later life he would serve on the Keighley Local Board of Health. At the age of six — twenty-nine years before — he had worked twelve and half hours a day in a cotton mill, with no time off for 'breakfast or drinking' ('I never knew a mill that had any time for breakfast or drinking in our neighbourhood'), and when 'there used to be a great call for cotton yarn', they would carry on till ten at night, till 'I was in such a state of stupor when I pieced an end, that I have had the skin taken off my fingers and hands; being asleep, as one may say, the frames went against my fingers'. He and his workmates used to sit on the window bottoms and fall asleep, 'and then the overlooker used to come and shake us by the ear, or give us a rap with the strap'. He used to fall asleep at Sunday School, too. When Firth was asked about early rising, his prose reached an eloquence transcending the occasion:

> ...When I talk to persons who have children going to factories, it makes my heart bleed; we cannot tell the tears which have been shed on those occasions; children are torn out of their bed in the morning; they have to encounter all weathers; they open the door and meet the snow-drift and the cold; and in these ways they have to undergo great suffering at a very tender age.

One is left with an abiding picture of Joseph Firth as a youth frightened of going crooked, 'and therefore I used constantly to make a spring up when I was working, to prevent my getting deformed'.

But saddest of the Keighley witnesses were two less fluent workingmen. Samuel Rhodes was nineteen in 1832, and had started work at six and a half 'at Mitchell's mill – a worsted mill', where the overlooker 'had a strap with nails in it'. ('Mr Mitchell,' John Hodgson assures us, 'was a gentleman highly respected by his workpeople and the public generally, and what was better still, we believe a genuine Christian'.) Aged eight, he had worked a thirteen and a quarter-hour day for machine-maker Berry Smith ('a gentleman very highly respected by his work-people and by all who had the pleasure of his acquaintance': Hodgson), where 'I began to be tired, and could not stand it; I got stiff in my limbs, and began growing deformed in my knees'.

'Will you,' his questioners asked, 'shew the gentlemen of the committee your limbs?' Whereupon Samuel Rhodes rolled up his trousers and 'appeared to be very crooked and knock-knee'd'. Out of thirty boys employed at Berry Smith's, he asserted, eight had deformed legs; crippled children abounded — 'in Keighley, you may find wagon-loads'.

Thomas Smith, a 27-year-old weaver, was only four feet eight inches tall. He had worked for three months in a cotton mill, but 'I was too little, I could not reach my work'. So, aged nine, he too had gone to Berry Smith's, had grown stiff in his legs, and dutifully showed the Committee his knees, which 'appeared much distorted' – his brother and sister were also crippled. His account of an accident suggests that factory children could still by nature be childish: 'the overlooker went out, and we were playing, two or three of us, taking the advantage while he was out, and as I was going by the upright shaft, it caught me by my clothes, and took me round; my left arm was broken in three places, and my head was sadly damaged...'

Michael Thomas Sadler lost his seat later in 1832, Lord Ashley taking his place as Parliamentary leader of the Ten Hours Movement. An 1833 Factory Act extended legislation to the textile industries, instituted government inspectors and factory schools, and fixed a maximum nine-hour working day for children aged nine to thirteen. An 1844 Act, whilst further restricting them to six and a half hours and advocating the fencing of machinery, actually lowered the minimum age

Child workers outside Haggas's Mill at Ingrow, 1908.

limit from nine to eight. But in 1847 John Fielden's Ten Hours Act (protecting, however, only young people and women) brought to fruition the campaigning of a generation of factory reformers.

Of course, Utopia was still a long way off. A vagueness as to dates of birth would necessitate, for years, Certificates of Age:

> 'I, John B. Beck, Surgeon, do hereby certify that Ann Robinson, Daughter of Selina Robinson residing in Keighley, has appeared before me, and submitted to my examination, and the said Ann Robinson is of the ordinary strength and appearance of a child at least NINE years of Age, As witness my hand this 10th day of July, 1844'.

Schooling would remain uneven, accidents commonplace – a mid-century letter-writer describes the death of Widow Sunderland, a weaver at Castle Mill: 'A Shaft got hold of her dress and werld her round 90 times in a minuit she was dead before they could stop the power'. But the Inspectors of Factories, albeit over-worked, were developing a keen eye for all manner of details:

> A common disease among factory children, and highly communicative from one to another, is scald head. It is generally concealed by the handkerchief which is worn under pretence of keeping the hair tidy – a practice which is not only exceedingly dangerous, but insanitary. All handkerchiefs worn on the head by children amongst machinery should be strictly forbidden, since several persons have been nearly strangled, and some have had the scalp torn off, by the ends of the handkerchiefs being caught among the flyers and wheels. A net is far more simple, more cleanly, and more comely....

Chapter Three

Keighley in 1823 – religious denominations – Savings Bank – Post Office – Select Vestry – Waterworks Act, 1816 – Keighley Improvement Act, 1824 – gas supply – fire brigade – poor relief

The community developing during the late eighteenth and early nineteenth centuries was centred on the High Street, Low Street and Church Green. A map of 1816 indicates buildings outward along the 'road to Skipton' and up the 'road from Cowling' (West Lane), with growing industrial property at Low Bridge and Greengate; but the Club Houses in King Street were still isolated, out along the 'road from Halifax', and Guard House comprised a few sprinkled dwellings. Fell Lane and Exley Head, Thwaites and Utley, were quite separate hamlets.

Edward Baines's Directory of 1823 describes Keighley as a 'considerable' market town, 'moderately' built 'almost wholly' of stone, with a population of 9,223 at the 1821 census. Object of pride, St Andrew's Church with its octagonal spire, eight bells and 'curious' clock made by Society of Arts prize-winner John Prior of Nessfield, had been rebuilt in 1805 – within forty years its roof would be falling in, and in 1846 it would be demolished. A strong Nonconformist element accounted for the existence of Quaker, Independent, Wesleyan, Swedenborgian, Baptist and Methodist New Connection places of worship.

The Society of Friends had been prominent in the district since the Commonwealth, holding to their faith despite imprisonment and confiscation of goods: 'Taken from T. Brigg, senior, tythe-corn for three years, £1 10s by the Priest of Keighley, 1679' ... Thomas Pearson of Keighley, for absenting from the National Worship ... committed to prison at York Jail, the 15th day of the first month, 1679, and remained several years'. Their meeting-house, built in 1690, stood near the High Street at Mill Hill.

The Dissenters or Independents had, by 1823, been worshipping as a church in Keighley for about a hundred years. Their first premises, a barn, had fallen down one Sunday night in 1760, and Upper Green Chapel, within a stone's-throw of the Friends' Meeting-House, was erected in 1820 on an earlier site.

The Swedenborgian temple in King Street, photographed about the turn of the century.

Both John and Charles Wesley had preached at Keighley in 1746, and sensing a happier spiritual climate than Heywood's seventy years earlier – 'Here also is the promise of a plentiful harvest' – became repeated visitors. Charles had 'about one thousand as well-behaved hearers as I have lately seen' in 1751, with another four thousand at Haworth; and John is credited with having harangued a crowd baiting a bull at Exley Head. Keighley's first Wesleyan Methodist Preaching House was opened in 1754 in Temple Row, enlarged in 1777, and replaced by a bigger Eden Chapel in 1811. In 1823 the Methodist New Connection also had a chapel in South Street, but by mid-century had sold out and split up.

The New Jerusalem or Swedenborgian doctrine had come early to the town, introduced in 1787; Keighley voices were heard at the first national New Church Conferences. In 1805 they built what they called their temple in King Street, with a text from Swedenborg above the door: 'All religion hath relation to life, and the life of religion is to do good' – Acres Mill, belonging to New Churchman Berry Smith, adjoined and eventually expanded round the temple. The Baptists too, after worshipping for several years in an upper room in Turkey Street, opened their chapel nearby in 1815; it would seat 'comfortably' a congregation of at least five hundred.

Baines's Directory suggests an active town with a wide range of trades. In addition to cotton and worsted manufacture, machine-making was emerging as a dominant industry. Richard Hattersley, like Berry Smith a New Churchman, had started making bolts and screws in 1789, having acquired Stubbing House Mill from yet another Swedenborgian, Joseph Wright. Within a few years he had progressed to rollers, spindles and flyers, and moved to North Brook Mill: his firm would begin to make power looms in 1834. Berry Smith (both he and Richard Hattersley became trustees of the Swedenborgian chapel in 1821) manufactured worsted spinning frames at Acres Mill, though he would eventually abandon this in favour of commission spinning. From his machine-shop in Low Street, Edward Carr was supplying frames as far afield as Cheshire and Cumberland. John and Samuel Smith had been burned out of Low Bridge Mill in 1821, but were soon determinedly turning out rollers, spindles and flyers from new premises at Long Croft; whilst William Smith & Sons had been making spinning frames since 1819.

Keighley also boasted four wool comb makers in 1823, with two reedmakers and four woolstaplers; three iron and brass founders, and one more specialised brass founder, John Vaux (who would soon go bankrupt); four braziers and tinsmiths, two nail makers and a paper maker; a thread manufacturer, and two rope makers. A period of feverish building activity was represented by seven stone masons, two timber merchants, ten joiners, three plasterers, three plumbers and glaziers, three house and sign painters; whilst the multiplying population was keeping some twenty grocers and ten tailors in business, together with sundry bakers, butchers, confectioners, earthenware dealers, boot and shoemakers, cloggers, tallow chandlers. .... Six of the joiners also described themselves as cabinet makers; and the finer side of living had occasioned two oil and colour dealers, three seedsmen, two hairdressers and perfumers, and three booksellers – one of whom, Robert Aked, ran a circulating library from his shop in Low Street. If a reliance on horses necessitated five blacksmiths, two saddlers and three wheelwrights, Keighley's two stay makers and three straw hat manufacturers remind us of the more attractive feminine fashions of the day.

Amongst five attornies appears the shadowy Christopher Netherwood, who would build the equally shadowy Cliffe Hall, precursor of Cliffe Castle. There were as many watch and clockmakers as doctors (four of each); and six rather grandly-named Academies: Thomas Plummer was currently master of the Free Grammar School; Mrs Atkinson and Miss Sharman were teaching girls; Edward Metcalfe laboured at classics and mathematics in Chapel Lane, Jesse Cawood at commerce in Chapel Fold; whilst the busy erstwhile Independent minister David Dewhirst (he had resigned his pastorate in 1821) kept a school in Mill Lane, as well as running a grocer's and a druggist's in the High Street. Another indefatigable citizen was David Illingworth of Church Street, who was hatter, hosier, draper and haberdasher, and even found time to man a Fire and Life Insurance Office for the Norwich Union. A handful of manufacturers – Isaac Butterfield, James and John Greenwood, William Sugden — had aspired to the titles of 'gentleman' or 'Esquire' and graduated into the Directory's 'Miscellany' section!

Some of these same gentlemen, together with clergy of the locality, were acting as trustees of the Savings Bank established in 1819. To be sure, this was as yet a humble concern, open only on Wednesdays from noon till two, Benjamin

Keighley's eighteenth-century Fleece Inn, replaced by a Marks and Spencer store in 1935.

Marriner at Greengate taking charge; but by 1826 it would carry a balance of over £3,500. Its Cash Book presents, amongst sick clubs and larger investors, the touching spectacle of smaller townsfolk putting by their odd shillings; and the trustees had a pleasant way of indicating progress by observing, for example, the number of female servants managing to save £10, or shopkeepers with £50.

Community life depended largely on Keighley's inns, which in the early nineteenth century represented more than drinking: meetings were held in them, friendly societies made them their headquarters, coroners sat on inquests. Church Street sported the Devonshire Arms, the Hole in the Wall, the King's Arms, the Rodney and the Sun; Low Street the Fleece, the Hare and Hounds, the Mason's Arms and the Black Horse – where Mrs Martha Cooke also kept the Post Office on a few shelves in the parlour, handing out letters through a hinged pane in the window. 'Well do I remember,' a later reminiscer would provide an inconsequential detail, 'a quaint old picture that hung on the wall outside, representing two men, one in gold-laced coat, cocked hat and wig, – the other in rags; the well-dressed man saying — by means of a label proceeding from his mouth — 'I shall go to law;' the other. pointing to his tattered vesture, replying 'I have been to law and won,' implying, it is to be supposed, that success had been his view'. Eighteenth-century mails had jogged in by saddlebag from Bradford three times a week, but by the 1820s there was a daily albeit 'shabby' mail gig, 'drawn by a jaded-looking horse, which leisurely trotted from Bradford to Keighley in the morning, and from Keighley to Bradford in the afternoon'. Its driver further slowed down the mails by carrying passengers at half-a-crown a head.

Travel was still a hazardous undertaking: one Keswick housekeeper took eight months screwing up her courage to visit her brother in Keighley, being meanwhile in a state of constant apprehension as to her health and the weather; then she was 'verry powerly' for ten days after the return trip. Her brother's 'beain Afraid my intended Jurney to youre plase would inger my helth' was no idle concern. In 1823, Keighley was served by two coaches, the *Royal Union* and the *Royal Alexander*, operating respectively from the Devonshire Arms and the Fleece; but many travelled more cheaply if slowly by carriers' cart. Wilkinson Lund set out from Low Street to Leeds on Monday mornings, returning on Tuesdays; and to Colne on Wednesdays and Bradford on Thursdays and Saturdays ... from Church Street, Sugden Pearson undertook a Colne return journey on Wednesdays ... James Wignall embarked for Skipton and Kettlewell at five o'clock on Monday mornings (he didn't get back till Wednesday night, in time to go to Halifax on Thursdays) ... John Cousin left for Manchester vaguely 'every week'.

Local government (such as it was) devolved upon the churchwardens, who appointed a variety of parish officers – overseers of the poor, surveyors of highways, constables, collectors of taxes. The crumbling minutes of Select Vestry meetings, liberally sprinkled with Greenwoods, Cravens and Claphams, Sugdens, Briggs and Haggases, Marriners and Hattersleys, show the rising industrialists prominent in public affairs; suggesting, too, men full of good resolves hampered by inadequate means. They planned to build a prison in 1815, but had to settle for 'a room or two to rent for a Lock up House' (not to exceed £5 per annum). The effect of their admirable determination, in 1799, that Keighley streets 'should be paved with dressed wall stones', is qualified by the amendment 'so far as the Surveyor can conveniently do in the year'. And always, of course, they were dealing with frail human nature: in 1822 it was discovered that 'for several Years back it has been the practice of the Surveyors of the Highways of the Township of Kighley to charge the Town with greater sums than they have actually paid'!

Yet the activities of the Select Vestry were many and various. They repaired bridges and scoured watercourses, ran the workhouse and (during the Napoleonic Wars) organised the militia ballot, took measures 'to cause the Sabbath to be more decently observed than heretofore in this Town and Parish', and launched a vigorous prosecution of James Bailey and his wife, of Thwaites, who committed 'a violent and outrageous assault upon William Wilkinson the younger of this Town in the due execution of his office as special Constable'.

The Select Vestry appointed parish constables from among its own members, and most of the town's more solid citizens served a year's term of office at one time or another. Law and order virtually depended on these unpaid, temporary and, one might imagine, over-worked amateurs distinguished only by their staffs embellished with the royal cipher. Their account-books indicate the multiplicity of their duties. They made a rather infrequent 'night round' inspecting public houses, apprehended men accused of bastardy (who had often fled into Lancashire), and arranged inquests:

March 1, 1816	'J. Bailey being killed at Ingrow pd. assistants bringing him to the first Inn and expenses of laying him out, 7s 6d.
March 3, 1816	'Charging jury, 6s. 'Journey to Skipton for Coroner, 5s. Pd. at inquest, £1. 1s.'

Constables attended to the adjusting of weights and measures, gave the bellman instructions for crying public announcements, and paid out casual relief to travelling paupers who included 'rogues and vagabonds', 'trampers', discharged soldiers and sailors, and soldiers' families and widows:

May 26, 1815	'Relieved a black Man (sick), 2s. Easter Bland for her trouble, 1s. 'Pd. Doctor Robinson for examining black man before I removed him, 5s. 'Paid for his Carriage to Denholme, 1s.'

Naturally, they were to the fore in emergencies, and were involved, for example, in 'searching all day in the river for a Boy drowned' or 'searching for Man supposed to have attempted entering John Peel's money Drawer'.

But a system, which might have worked adequately for a small community, could not continue indefinitely in a rapidly increasing town. In 1816, in an effort to come more effectively to grips with a specific problem, a number of residents – who included such familiar names as John Greenwood, William Sugden, Berry Smith, Thomas Corlass, David Illingworth and the Rector, the Revd Theodore Dury – formed a Company of Proprietors of Keighley Waterworks and obtained an Act of Parliament for 'better supplying with water the inhabitants of the town of Keighley'.

Keighley, as its preamble pointed out, 'has of late years become very populous, and is greatly increased in Houses and Buildings' (the population was in process of swelling from the 6,864 of 1811 to the 9,223 of 1821); yet the principal water supply depended on Jennet's and Whin Knowle Wells, to the west at Black Hill, and Park Springs to the north-east. The Company of Proprietors proposed to construct 'Pipes, Drains, Aqueducts, and Conduits, under-ground Works, and other Conveniences above-ground for conveying the Water of the Said Wells or Springs ... towards and unto the said Town'. They raised the necessary finances by issuing 143 shares at £25 each, and work began the following year. A quarter of a century later, most Keighley households were within reach of a stand-pipe, at least; though the water supply tended to be irregular, and sometimes in summer was turned on for only two hours a day.

A general inadequacy of public amenities led, in 1824, to the formation of a governing body somewhat optimistically named the Keighley Improvement Commissioners, appointed by an Act of Parliament 'for paving, lighting, cleansing, watching, regulating, and otherwise improving the Town of Keighley', and assuming, in effect, responsibilities previously exercised by the churchwardens – some of whom automatically became Commissioners: their first meetings continued to be held in the vestry. To qualify for office, a Commissioner had to be worth at least £1,000, and a catalogue of those of 1824 suggests where the means and the power in Keighley lay: William Barrett, John Barker, George Beck, John Brigg, Isaac Butterfield, Lodge Calvert, William Cockshott, Joshua Cowling, Thomas Corlass, John Craven, Robert Dawson, the Revd Theodore Dury, William Ellis, Frederick and Edwin Greenwood, Richard Hattersley, Hugh Heaton, David Illingworth, Benjamin Flesher Marriner and William Marriner, John Ramsden, Berry, John and Thomas Smith, William Sugden, George Taylor, Francis Topham, John Town and William Weatherhead. They include the Rector, a doctor (Beck), and a couple of shopkeepers (Illingworth and Weatherhead); but the main strength lies with the manufacturers.

The Improvement Act extended to 'all such Parts of the Parish of Keighley as are within One Mile from the Spot where the old Cross stood, immediately adjoining the North-east Corner of the Devonshire Arms Inn'. Briefly, it envisaged streets and entries paved, drained and lit 'either by Oil Lamps, or by means of Gas or Inflammable Air', patrolled at night by watchmen and regularly swept of 'Dirt, Dust, Soil, Dung, Manure, and Filth': to be financed (of course) by the levying of 'One or more Rate or Rates, Assessment or Assessments, once or oftener in every Year upon the Tenants or Occupiers of all Dwelling Houses, Shops, Workhouses, Workshops, Mills, Warehouses, Coach-houses, Stables, and other Buildings'. Interesting clauses forbade river pollution during the manufacture of gas, and imposed a £5 fine or three months' hard labour on anybody caught wilfully breaking lamps.

The Commissioners undertook, moreover, an overall policing of the town. For probably the first time, the 1824 Act presented Keighley residents with a set of increasingly necessary regulations and restrictions: you were no longer allowed to push barrows, roll tubs or drive cattle along pavements, nor set up stalls or hang out washing so as to obstruct passers-by. Animals were not to be killed in the streets, unless being destroyed after accidents, nor exposed for sale, except during the Fair. You were forbidden to light bonfires in public places, let off squibs, fire guns, play football, cut up meat, drive carts without reins or ride horses 'furiously'. Carcases and offal were not to be dumped in wells. If you had a flower-pot at your window, it was to be secure; and if you kept a dog, and the town crier gave notice of suspected rabies, it was to be muzzled. This last, incidentally, was a serious consideration. At a time when deaths from hydrophobia were far from uncommon the cry 'Mad dog!' roused a peculiar horror. As diarist Abraham Shackleton of Braithwaite records, on three February days in 1794: 'A mad Dog came through Braithwaite, I followed it to Laycock … Ran Mad Dog again to Paper Mill. It wasn't killed … Ran a mad dog this afternoon it got killed at R. Aire.'

The Improvement Act, of course, represented an ideal which the Commissioners were largely unable to translate into reality. One aspect in which they were singularly successful, however, was lighting. By their second meeting, they were investigating 'Plans and Estimates of the Expences of Lighting the Town of Keighley with Coal or Oil Gas'. Eighteen energetic months later, they had built Gas Works on land purchased from Lord George Cavendish at Low Bridge, had ordered 'two boat load of Bierley best bed of Coal', and had undertaken, not only to supply public street lamps, but also to sell gas to mills and individuals. Keighley became gas-lit in November, 1825, with 93 public lamps, the siting of which suggests, still, a community of familiars: 'Cook Lane Corner of Plumbing shop ... Beecrofts Coal Corner lowside ... Near Midgley shop door ... High Corner Independent Chapel yard ... Widow Wright corner ... Thos. Corlass house Sisters high Window.' The following March – symbolic of a shift from churchwarden government – Commissioners' meetings transferred their venue from the vestry to the Gas Office at Low Bridge.

As with all innovations, there were difficulties. Consumers using jet burners (there were few meters in the early days) enlarged the holes, thereby 'causing them to give almost as much Light for 10s 6d as Five-Hole Argand Burners at 22s 6d.' £99 5s 8d had to be written off due to 'the destruction of Retorts by want of experience'. Stated an indignant placard in July, 1827: 'The Total Consumption of Gas in Twenty-four Hours in January last, at the Dark of the Moon, was 7,000 feet, viz. 3,000 feet in the Streets, and in the Shops 4,000 feet. The Commissioners only received payment for 2,400 feet; leaving 1,600 feet in the Twenty-four Hours, for which nothing was paid; being a loss of 16s each night to the Rate Payers'. Gradually, however, with increased sale of gas by meters, the financial situation improved.

In May of 1829 the Commissioners turned their attention to another responsibility: 'Ordered That a new Engine House shall be erected to contain the Fire Engine which has been purchased by Subscription from Wm. Lawson – and Messrs. Greenwoods and Claytons Engines – these Gentlemen having agreed to deposit them at the Gas works'; the latter being private mill engines which their owners, Messrs. John Greenwood & Sons and William Clayton of Low Mill, were making available for public use. All three were housed at the Gas Works, whence they could be quaintly 'obtained on application' at the rate of ten shillings per hour. Six firemen were appointed, two for each engine, and required to spend a modest two hours every three months in cleaning their apparatus, for which duty they were paid an equally modest four shillings a year (they had to be cautioned about 'using any impertinence or importunity in soliciting for subscriptions at Christmas'). They got sixpence an hour when attending fires, and were distinguished by a 'leather label' in the fronts of their hats, inscribed 'Keighley Fire Man'; the doors of their homes – presumably for the benefit of frantic burning householders – were likewise embellished with a board announcing 'Keighley Fire Man'.

Their first recorded call seems to have come in December, 1829, when an engine 'proved of great service' at a fire on the premises of a Mr Longbottom of Silsden; this must have been a lengthy affair, since the charge was £3 for the engine and three shillings each for the firemen. Silsden, it will be noted, lay outside the limits of the Keighley Improvement Act – a point which was raised again, on January 3rd 1831:

> The Commissioners have learnt with great concern on assembling this day that a messenger arrived about 9 o'clock yesterday morning from Skipton, with an account of Mr Dewhirst's Cotton & Worsted Factory being on Fire and that all the three Engines with the Firemen were instantly dispatched – that one of them broke down on the Road, but that the other two arrived at Skipton in 40 minutes after leaving Keighley and were happily instrumental in saving Mr Dewhirst's steam Engine.

Mr Dewhirst's bill for this service amounted to £16 0s 6d; the Commissioners also made an abortive overture to his insurance companies 'for a liberal compensation for the use of the Engines and as a remuneration to the Men'. Most important, however, was a stipulation that in future no more than two of the three engines should leave the town at once.

An idea of the apparatus may be gleaned from a minute of 1840, when one engine was found to be 'compleatly perished and rotten in the wood part, and that owing to its being made in that peculiar way as to render it extremely difficult to turn, it was ordered to be repaired that is a good substantial new body made, to fit exactly the iron work, made to turn on a pivot between the front wheels, and with a pair of shafts so that a horse when required may be attached'. Five years later a new engine was bought for £100. Nicknamed the 'Water Witch', it was complete with 'hose, suction and conducting pipes, with drivers seat on springs and spoke wheels'. In 1846, the Halifax, Bradford and Keighley Insurance Company agreeing to pay half the expenses, the firemen were increased to twelve, provided with uniforms and new buckets, and given half-a-crown each at Christmas 'in lieu of begging'. What was more to the purpose, they drilled monthly instead of quarterly, whilst a bell was fixed at Low Bridge 'to give notice for their immediate attendance at the works in case of fire'.

In other respects the Commissioners were less happy. Their Act had authorised them 'to appoint such Number of able-bodied Men as they shall judge proper to be employed as Watchmen'; but, though they hired two in October, 1828, they discharged them with the approach of lighter nights the following April. Watchmen themselves were notoriously suspect (the Improvement Act had threatened a forty-shilling fine on alehouse-keepers 'harbouring' them during their hours of duty); but Keighley's short-lived guardians of the peace did at least report that 'Banks Booth of the Wool Pack Inn, keeps a very disorderly House'. The Gas Works superintendent was tamely instructed to 'call upon Mr Booth to request him to be more circumspect for the future, otherwise the Commissioners will be under the painful necessity of noticing it'. A decade later they were still without watchmen, feeling themselves unable to 'saddle the works with so heavy a charge'. Not till the winter of 1842 were two more permanent watchmen appointed at a salary of fifteen shillings a week each. The number was increased to four in 1848.

The Commissioners' attitude towards the general regulating of the town was similarly cautious. When, in 1829, one Mary Smith and her son built a wall which neighbours alleged was 'an encroachment upon the rights of the public and an obstruction to the Road', the following minute was carefully framed:

> The removal of encroachments and nuisances being clearly within the powers of the Commissioners, they are disposed to interfere in the case in question, by instituting an enquiry into the matter, but as the state of the funds do not admit of any additional burdens it is hereby ordered, that in case the owners of the property adjoining give the Commissioners a satisfactory undertaking to pay all the expences that may be incurred, they will then take the necessary legal steps.

Paving, too, was neglected. Anomalously, highways remained the responsibility of the surveyors appointed by the Select Vestry, and the Commissioners – whose rating authority extended only to buildings and not to land – were content to delegate any ambiguous powers their Act might have given them in this respect.

Another responsibility continuing in the churchwardens' hands was the relief of the poor. Miles Gale had noted Keighley's numerous paupers, together with the benefactions on their behalf. Isaac Bowcock, a Tong stapler with land at Utley, had by his will of 1669 left £25 a year for 'putting out Five Poor Men's Sons Apprentices', supplying the necessitous, and 'setting up, in Trades and Stocks, such as are hopeful'. Isabel Hall in 1633, and George Clapham in 1681, had each left £1 a year for the poor; John Clapham, £1 16s in 1686. At Haworth in 1723, David Midgley of Withens had made provision for clothing ten poor children a year: boys to have 'a coat, waistcoat, and breeches of blue cloth, a blue cloth cap, and a pair of stockings'; girls 'a blue cloth jacket, two petticoats, a blue cap, and a pair of blue stockings'.

Such charity, of course, had barely skimmed the surface of poverty in a landscape of hard farming and risky cottage industry; the main burden of relief being met by a rate levied on householders and administered by Overseers of the Poor appointed by the parish authorities. The destitute from other parishes living in Keighley were despatched – to keep local rates down – to those chargeable for their upkeep (other parishes likewise returning Keighley's wandering poor). Pauper children were apprenticed and able-bodied adults set to work; but, though Keighley did boast a workhouse at Exley Head, relief largely took the form of goods and money intended to help the needy struggle on in their own homes: 'Ordered that James Judson be allowed 2s per week … that Rachel Green have cotton for a shift … that John Wright be allowed a double truss & 7s 6d towards fitting up a pair of looms … that John Waring have cloth allowed for a shirt … that Marshall's Child be allowed 20s towards a pair of looms as soon as it begins to weave … that Joseph Walbank Widow be allowed 10s towards her rent….'

By the early decades of the nineteenth century, high prices, the long French wars, and the rapidly growing industrial population had magnified the problem of poverty. Joseph Shackleton, a boy in Keighley in the 1820s, would recall a diet of porridge and potatoes, 'with a little fat now and again. We often had porridge three or four times a day. If we could only get a little old milk and treacle with it we used to consider we had quite a treat. But mostly we had to take it without. This oatmeal porridge was about the only food poor people could afford, besides potatoes, and in order to get even that they had to work very hard'. One winter he had to wear a bit of old sheet instead of a jacket; his bed had consisted of straw and shavings on the floor. He had seen families of six and seven living in a single room.

The Poor Law Amendment Act of 1834 sought to regularise what had become a nationally uneven system of relief, by taking responsibility from parishes and substituting Unions, each administered by a Board of Guardians answerable to a central Poor Law Commission. Outdoor relief was discouraged, greater emphasis being placed on the heavily institutionalised charity of the workhouse, whereby the poor tended to become degraded and to lose their sense of independence. In the event, outdoor relief continued; but the Act aroused bitter opposition. A meeting of 'principal inhabitants' of Keighley in 1834 sent petitions to both Houses of Parliament on the grounds that 'the delegation of the powers to the [Poor Law] Commissioners to make Rules & Laws & have the principal Control in administering the Funds for the Relief of the Poor is wholly unconstitutional, & ought to remain as at present under the Control of the Ratepayers'. As late as 1837, a public meeting, so well attended that it had to move out of the vestry into the Market, was debating 'the Propriety of taking Measures for procuring a suspension of the Order for forming of the Keighley Union of the Poor Law'. When a Poor Law Commissioner came to implement the Act, he was manhandled by a crowd demonstrating outside the Mechanics' Institute.

Ultimately, of course, the Keighley Union was formed, embracing a wider area than that of the town or parish, and including Bingley, Micklethwaite, Morton, Haworth, Steeton, Eastburn and Sutton. Its Board of Guardians numbered sixteen, and its first relieving officer was that same poetical Abraham Wildman who had testified to the Sadler Committee in 1832.

The relieving officer saw the sad side of life indeed; everyone in need represented a personal misery or misfortune: 'Old and Infirm' ... 'Imbecility' ... 'Weak in intellect' ... 'Subject to fits' ... 'Debility' ... 'Blind and Daughter weak in intellect' ... 'Cripple' ... 'Lame' ... 'Orphans' ... 'Unable to support her bastard children' ... 'Husband absconded' ... 'Husband gone for a Soldier' ... 'Part in prison and sickness'.

Pauper documentation provides a moving revelation of the small people whom history forgets. Said 39-year-old Elizabeth Rhodes, broken by too many children and typhus fever in 1838: 'My husband went to America seven years ago. I believe he is dead, I have heard so, many times'. Vociferated a not entirely grammatical Wildman in 1840, writing to the Burley Overseers about 'Fredk. Metcalfes Wife':

> She is now recovered and able to come over to you and unless the Bill of the Expences now incurred in her behalf within 4 days is paid we shall take out an order for her and

> her Family's Removal. I have had two persons to attend her one of whom caught the Fever and is now laying dead leaving a Family of 4 children to lament their irreparable loss caused entirely through your paupers residence here & we are determined to quit this Town of an Idle, disorderly & profligate Female and losing her to her own place of Settlement.

Saddest of all were the bastardy investigations, attempts to trace unwilling fathers:

> The evidence of Martha Mosley taken this day the 18th Dec. 1837 – touching the case of Mary Mosley's child – 'I am 25 years of age. I have known John Hey for these last 12 years – It is now 4 years since he came acourting to my sister – I have many times seen them together with his arms around her waist. I have seen them in the evenings at all times – say from 8 to 10 – before she was pregnant and many times since – My sister has often told me that he promised her marriage – he frequently came into our house – both in the day time and the night – Some times they went out into the fold. He used to leave the house on a night about 10 or eleven – He promised my sister a Soverin — for her expences during her confinement and I went up to see if he would give her something towards the same but he gave me nothing – He told me he would allow her a Shilling a week for the Child...'

Sometimes Abraham Wildman jotted down his scraps of verse on the back of his official papers. One pencilled stanza begins: 'I have no hope — but deep despair...'

Chapter Four

Keighley Mechanics' Institute – schools – Butterworth Panic – churches and chapels – Masons and Oddfellows – societies – travel – manufacturers – Corn Laws – strikes and poverty

One Saturday night, January 22nd 1825, John Farish, a reed-maker who lived in Upper Green, had three friends in for what was then ponderously termed 'social intercourse': John Bradley, a house and sign painter, William Dixon, a tailor, and John Haigh, a joiner. One of them (local history does not record which) had got hold of a copy of *The Mechanics' Magazine* describing 'the establishment and progress of a society formed by the operatives of the Gas Company in Glasgow', which so impressed them that they forthwith appointed themselves as chairman, secretary and committee of two for 'a society for mutual instruction, and to establish a library for that purpose'. Thirteen attended a discussion two days later – again at Farish's – and on February 14th a public meeting, in the hired room constituting the National School, adopted the rules which launched the Keighley Mechanics' Institute. The following month, Edward Baines, junior, who had helped found the Leeds Mechanics' Institute the previous year, lectured its first members on 'the most effectual means' of developing their project. In the gathering momentum of the Mechanics' Institute movement in the north of England, Keighley was well to the fore.

The locality had seen an earlier experiment in adult education, a glimpse of which has survived, slenderly, through the manuscript diary kept by Abraham Shackleton, of Braithwaite, aged eighteen at the time. On March 17th, 1794, he had written: 'We begun our school for reading Grammar this Night'; and during subsequent days added a few details: 'We had our school at Braithwaite this Night, & we subscribed everyone a shilling to our Library 16 of us. The school was appointed to be held twice a week, on Mon. nights at Calversikehill and on Thur. Nights at Braithwaite'. Shackleton seems to have been helping to build up this library – 'Went to Ky. with Wm. Wright & carried Volume of odd Magazines & Shipwreck of Antelope & got Town & Country Mag. for 1786 & Binns Catalogue

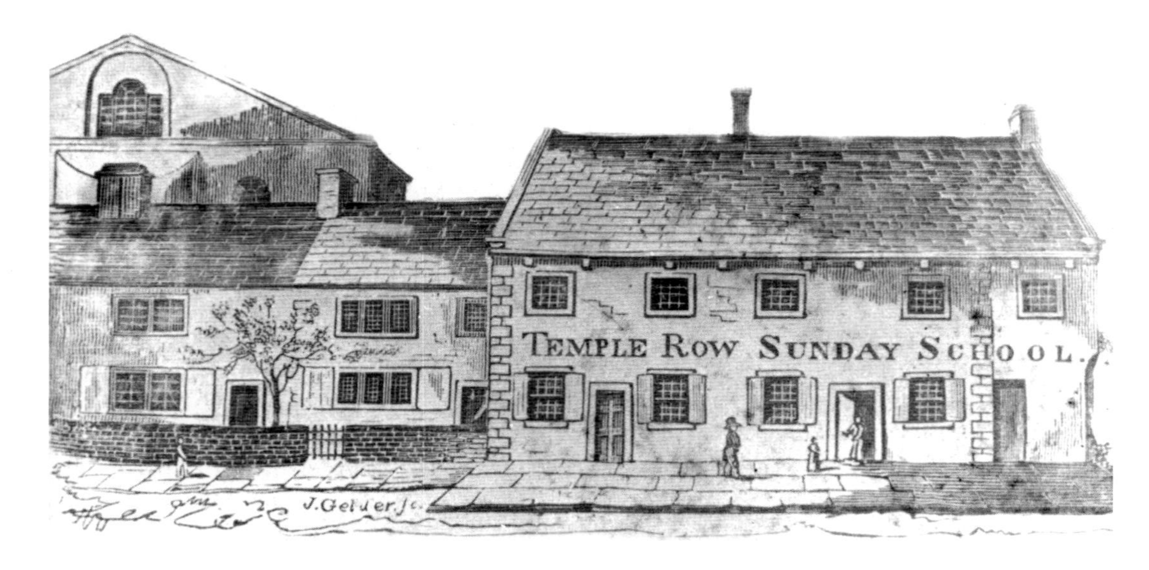

The Temple Row Sunday School in the early nineteenth century.

for 1789'. Other books he mentions are two volumes of a history of England, and 'Walker's Dictionary & Chesterfields advice to his son'. He also notes having been 'to Whin Knowle to look at stars through F. Waterhouses Perspective Glass'.

Early nineteenth-century education was in parlous circumstances. Keighley's five 'academies' of the 1820s offered only a limited tuition to a financially restricted clientele. The Sadler Committee's evidence suggests that any Sunday Schools grappling, however tentatively, with elementary teaching, faced a hopeless task; though in 1821 the Temple Row Wesleyan Methodist Sunday School was introducing reading and writing to a staggering 815 children of all denominations. The Free Grammar School boasted only fifty pupils in 1827, by which time John Drake's estate was proving scarcely adequate to pay the master's £100 per year salary. The National Church School was as yet struggling on in a hired room at Mill Hill – not till 1835 would its West Lane buildings open.

Probably the outer villages fared rather better. The Harehills Free School at Oakworth had been endowed by Sarah Heaton in 1738, and took in boarders (who were fed 'no meat, but bacon collops and puddings as hard as lead'). The Haworth Free Grammar School, founded by Christopher Scott in 1638 and situated at Marsh, was enlarged in 1818 and accommodated two hundred scholars by 1827. Its master was 'competent to teach Latin', but spent much of his time and energy dinning the alphabet into 'extremely young' children – John Kitson, it will be recalled, had attended for a year before he was five. At Stanbury, a school had been built by public subscription in 1805, and twenty years later some sixty children were learning 'reading, writing, and accounts', albeit in rough and ready fashion: 'Facing the scholars, the master had what we call a spindle chair, and in front of him was a three-legged table. On this table at times there were a dozen sticks that he had got out of the woods, and when any scholar was inattentive he would throw one of these sticks, and scarcely ever did he miss the child aimed at. During prayers more sticks went than at any other time'.

Into this most uncertain educational climate the Mechanics' Institute brought – at twopence a week and a five-shilling entrance fee – to the more coherent working man, a promise of higher things. Their earliest activities, in a borrowed room at the Grammar School, may sound tame to modern ears –'the members met during two evenings of the week, viz. – Monday and Friday, from eight to ten o'clock. The first hour of the four was spent in collecting the weekly contributions; the remaining three were occupied by the renewal of books, conversations, essays, or readings from such periodicals as the 'Mechanics' Magazine' and others of a more literary character; occasional lectures were also given by the members, as well as by professional lecturers' – but to men busy the day long, doors hitherto undreamt-of were opening. As the first Annual Report of the Keighley Mechanics' Institute declaims: 'Latent genius may be excited and prompted to action. The dormant abilities of individuals, yet unknown, may be roused, brought to light, improved, and exerted for the general good'.

Though conceived by working men and intended primarily for the benefit of humbler residents, the Keighley Mechanics' Institute could not have advanced far, once money was involved, without the industrialists and professional class. Heading its first list of donors (£2 and upwards) were John, Edwin and Frederick Greenwood, William Sugden and the Revd Theodore Dury, Berry Smith, Samuel Clapham, the Marriners, Lodge Calvert, and Simeon Townend of Ebor Mill. A little lower down (£1) came two doctors, George Beck and John Mitchell; Messrs. Hattersley and Sons; the former Independent minister David Dewhirst; and Abraham Shackleton, who had experienced its forerunner in 1794. Beck and Mitchell also donated, respectively, *Thompson's Chemistry, 4 Vols.* and *Cook's Voyages, 3 Vols.* Thomas Teal, collector of the water rate, gave *Seneca's Morals*; and eccentric James Mitchell of Oldfield (the 'old gentleman' who would be buried in his own field), an eminently practical *Banks' Treatise on Mills; and Banks, on the Power of Machines*. By the end of its first year, the Mechanics' Institute had 150 volumes in its library, together with an electrifying machine donated by Hugh Heaton. Out of seventy-one members, 'twenty-six have ceased paying, and eight have paid their entrance-money and no more'.

The Mechanics' Institute had formed in an unpropitious hour. 1825 witnessed the bitter Bradford woolcombers' strike and Keighley manufacturers' hostility to Union workers; 1826 brought financial disaster. National over-speculation, backed by a proliferation of small private banks, suddenly crashed in the face of rising home prices and booming imports: during the opening weeks of 1826, more than sixty banks stopped payment. In the West Riding, the collapse was named after the hapless firm – Messrs. Butterworth – which was first to fail; fifty years later, old people were still referring to the Butterworth Panic 'with bated breath, as if they were talking of one of the world's calamities'.

Probably Hodgson exaggerates in alleging that 'the majority of the Keighley tradesmen were ruined'. Nonetheless, failure and retrenchment were rife. At Castle Mill, Abraham Sugden saw 'all his spare cash' swept away; stated one bankrupt: 'I went into business with £700 in good money, and now after struggling hard for a number of years I am a ruined man'; William Wilkinson, who had built a worsted mill in South Street, lost £14,000 and died in the workhouse. The Mechanics' Institute's first Annual Report had sad cause to bemoan 'the present unprecedented commercial distress, and consequent pecuniary embarrassments of the operative classes of society'.

Worse, for the Institute, was to come: 'so far had its interests declined' in 1827 that no Report was issued, no public meetings held; members withdrew, subscriptions fell off. Amongst those doggedly lecturing such fellow-members as would listen, through this trying period, were founders John Farish on electricity, and John Haigh on the mechanical powers. By 1828, the Mechanics' Institute had narrowly weathered the storm, with forty-one subscribing members (a further sixty-eight had fallen behind on their weekly payments) and 263 library books, together with sundry scientific apparatus; and the following year's Report was able to state that 'the Society was never in a more prosperous condition'. Members delivering lectures included the Revd Theodore Dury (zoology), John Bradley (the steam engine), David Dewhirst (the properties of bodies), and John Mitchell (respiration). It was scarcely appealing to the 'operative' class, however – its 106 members in 1830 show a strong bias towards manufacturers, shopkeepers and artisans, with a sprinkling of clergy and professional men.

Thenceforth, the development of the Keighley Mechanics' Institute would be, in the main, a success story. In 1834 its pleasant little building was erected in North Street (John Greenwood & Sons the largest subscribers with £20), its library, classes and meetings coming under the same roof from scattered locations in the Free Grammar School, the Savings Bank, the Wesleyan School and the Court House. It must be admitted that highly educational public meetings seldom proved successful – 'Mr Addams' Lectures on Acoustics' in 1835 netted only £6 8s 1d in admission takings, whilst Mr Addams' fee was £21. The money-spinners turned out to be the visit of a New Zealand chief and 'Mrs Crowther's Performance on Musical Glasses'.

The Mechanics' Institute librarian received £5 per annum, and had the option of 'the two Rooms under the Library & Reading room' at £5 rent; he was also expected to 'erect the stage' and 'attend at the door' for lectures. Ten years after its establishment, the library boasted more than eight hundred volumes ranging over philosophy, history, natural history, geography, arts and sciences, poetry and general literature. The Committee had felt the necessity of buying some balloting balls, due to a delicate situation whereby there were several booksellers in the town, one of whom, James Aked, was on the Committee: 'Proposed that Chas. Crabtree have the order of Books selected this evening, but the balls turned in favour of Mr Aked therefore the order was given to him'.

None of the Institute's four founders took an especially prominent part in its subsequent progress. Haigh and Dixon soon disappeared from its activities. John Farish continued sporadically on its Committee for some years, but the minutes

Above left: *John Farish (1785-1858), from a portrait possibly by John Bradley.*

Above: *'Mr Craven's walk mill' – a John Bradley drawing of 1820.*

Left: *John Bradley (1787-1844), a self-portrait.*

show him to have been largely absent or silent, and his office of Inspector of Apparatus was not an unqualified success – a delegation had 'to call upon Mr Farish late inspector of apparatus to account for certain apparatus that are missing'. Yet his had been the driving force of 1825 (his membership number was 1). This son of a Scots packman, with his dour warty face and most of his ten children dying in infancy, was the perfect ascetic. He regarded the reading of novels as 'only another kind of mischievous excitement', doggedly teaching himself arithmetic, algebra, mensuration, trigonometry, geometry, mechanics, electricity, galvanism, hydrostatics, pneumatics, chemistry and optics; he could make barometers; he understood clockwork, telescopes and microscopes. For forty years he took in a few pupils to share his nightly studies, and when he died, aged seventy-two in 1858, over two hundred of them paid his funeral expenses.

John Bradley, the house and sign painter who acted as the Mechanics' Institute's first secretary, was also a competent artist and recorded a number of graphic Keighley scenes. His picture of the Airedale Heifer at East Riddlesden Hall – she weighed '41 stones 12 lbs. per quarter, 16 lbs. to the stone, and measured 11 feet 10 inches from her nose to the stump of the tail, and 10 feet 6 inches in girth' – found its way as an engraving into many Northern inn parlours. A more enthusiastic Committee member than Farish, Bradley abandoned his office as Vice-President of the Institute in order to emigrate with his family to America in 1831.

In Philadelphia he endured a winter so cold that water froze in buckets in the same room as a fire. 'The women,' he wrote home, 'are generally handsome, and they know it; in summer they go without stays, which detracts from their figure, making them appear all of a thickness, like a round dumpling'. By 1833, disillusioned with the New World, he had returned to Keighley, and was described as the architect of the North Street Mechanics' Institute building, the accounts of which include his bills 'for painting outside'. He died in 1844.

Possibly the predominating influence, throughout the first decade and a half of the Mechanics' Institute, was Keighley's scholarly Rector from 1814 to 1840, the Revd Theodore Dury, a contemporary of Byron at Harrow and a graduate of Pembroke College, Cambridge. For some years he edited a children's magazine, *The Monthly Teacher* (printed by Robert Aked of Low Street). He experimented with electricity, finding that 'when a leathern strap passed over two drums and crossed midway, so as to resemble the figure 8, singular electrical effects were exhibited at the point of crossing'; and corresponded with Faraday on the subject. His numerous services to the Institute included ordering library books when he travelled to London on business.

Meanwhile, the community, in time to the accelerating pulse of the nineteenth century, was developing in many directions. Places of worship were in process of achieving their dominance of the West Riding townscape. The Protestant Methodists, who had broken away from the Wesleyans, opened their Sun Street Chapel in 1831; the Roman Catholics their St Anne's Church in 1838, designed by Augustus Welby Pugin who would decorate the interior of the Houses of Parliament.

Nonconformism flourished, especially in neighbouring villages. There had been a Baptist chapel in West Lane, Haworth, since 1752; in 1825, members who had withdrawn after a dispute 'over musick' (as one diarist succinctly records) built their Particular Baptist Chapel at Hall Green. The Slack Lane Baptists formed in 1819, Horkinstone in 1836. The Wesleyan Methodists opened chapels at Lowertown, Oxenhope, in 1805, Haworth in 1816, Stanbury in 1832, Ingrow in 1840, Morton in 1846, and Hainworth in 1847; whilst the classical dignity of their Temple Street Chapel dates from 1846. In 1827, the Primitive Methodists built a chapel at Morton; followed by others at Mill Hey, Haworth, in 1836, Queen Street, Keighley, in 1837, and Riddlesden in 1843. The Independents or Congregationalists gained a footing at Morton in 1845 and Utley the following year.

Lagging slightly behind the Nonconformists, the Church of England too came to the out-districts. Ingrow St John's was consecrated in 1843. The following year, another St John's acquired two rooms as a chapel of ease in the seventeenth-century Church Farm at Newsholme. Christ Church, Oakworth, followed in 1846, St Mary the Virgin, Oxenhope, in 1849 – earlier Oxenhope worshippers had attended Haworth's St Michael's Church, rebuilt in 1755 on a fourteenth-century site. St Mary's at Riddlesden and St Luke's at Morton opened respectively in 1850 and 1851; Keighley's own St Andrew's Church being rebuilt in the Perpendicular style between 1846 and 1848. One of the manuscript autobiographers whose

Temple Street Wesleyan Methodist Chapel, c. *1890.*

reminiscences clothe the bare bones of history, has left a pleasant picture of local Parish Church attendance at this period:

> People came from miles around to the services on Sunday. They often brought food with them, but they could obtain food also from the many inns clustered round the church. Broth, with dumpling, cost a penny a basin, but only a halfpenny without. Country folks would come in pattens along the muddy roads to keep their shoes and white stockings clean. They carried white aprons to put on at the church door and a white handkerchief in their hands.

Freemasonry had enjoyed an unobtrusive authority in the district since the late eighteenth century. Keighley's Royal Yorkshire Lodge – instigated by local Masons initiated in the Royal Lancashire Lodge at Colne – received its Warrant in 1788 and met at the Devonshire Arms, later removing to the Lord Rodney, where landlord and Mason William Fox 'fit up a private room for the Lodge meetings', the Lodge finding 'its own coals and light' but paying no rent. During the French wars, militiamen and soldiers were admitted at half-price; and membership lists up to the mid-1800s show a cross-section of trades, cotton and worsted manufacturers and machine-makers, like Henry Clapham, William Wilkinson, Robert Stell and Richard Hattersley (Worshipful Master in 1805) rubbing shoulders with weavers and woolcombers and farmers. The Three Graces Lodge, formed at Barnoldswick in 1792, moved to the Black Bull, Haworth, in 1806 – John Farish received his first degree here in 1815 – later transferring to the King's Arms. On September 8th, 1831, both Lodges, complete with regalia, marched in procession to celebrate the coronation of William IV.

The Independent Order of Oddfellows founded their Loyal Eboracum Lodge in Keighley in 1823, meeting at the Commercial Inn. According to their centenary historian, 'the establishment resulted from the efforts of a number of working men, chiefly hand woolcombers, who were advanced politicians, chartists and the like' – certainly, one founder member was comber Joseph Firth, who would testify to the Sadler Committee. Formed, like the Mechanics' Institute, at a time of trade depression, the Eboracum Lodge made a slow start; but by 1835, with nearly a hundred members, acquired its own premises in Cross Leeds Street, still on the outskirts of town near the Baptist Chapel and the National School.

If the spirit of a community can be gauged by its societies, Keighley was becoming a lively place. In 1835 came a Horticultural Society, holding annual exhibitions; whilst the Revd Theodore Dury founded a Temperance Society, 'on the moderation principle' but moving towards a militant total abstinence as the Victorian era progressed. A Choral Society followed in 1837, and met in the Baptist schoolroom for a decade before moving into the Infant Room at the National School. The few surviving pages of the choir's minute-book detail their efforts to 'get up an Oratorio' early in 1847, when 'being short of Treble Singers, it was moved that Mrs Peace of Huddersfield be wrote to, to ask her if she would come and upon what terms, which was done accordingly, and her answer was she would be glad to come at the time and her Terms would be a Guinea & a half and her expences at Keighley, which offer was accepted, it was still thought adviseable to have more Treble, consequently Mr Wm. Robinson was requested to see what could be had from Bradford which he did accordingly and engaged Isaac White a Bass Singer to come and bring 2 Trebles with him for one Pound. Thomas Carrodus was afterwards asked to come and lead which he agreed to and bring his Son with him for Twelve Shillings and a few others about the Town was engaged'. Unpaid performers were rewarded with a supper which 'terminated in a loss to the Society' as the committee responsible ordered too generously ('it will be well in future always to be rather under than over').

In 1842 John Greenwood Sugden, son of William Sugden of Eastwood House and Fleece Mill but gentleman-farmer by inclination, offered, as 'an inducement to the operative to save the money which he otherwise might spend in the beerhouse', a prize for the best pig bred by a workman in his employment: from which, the following year, grew the first Keighley Agricultural Show. Pig-breeding was a popular hobby of the period – it was an Exley Head weaver, Joseph Tuley, who perfected the Large White Yorkshire which carried off, among others, 'the

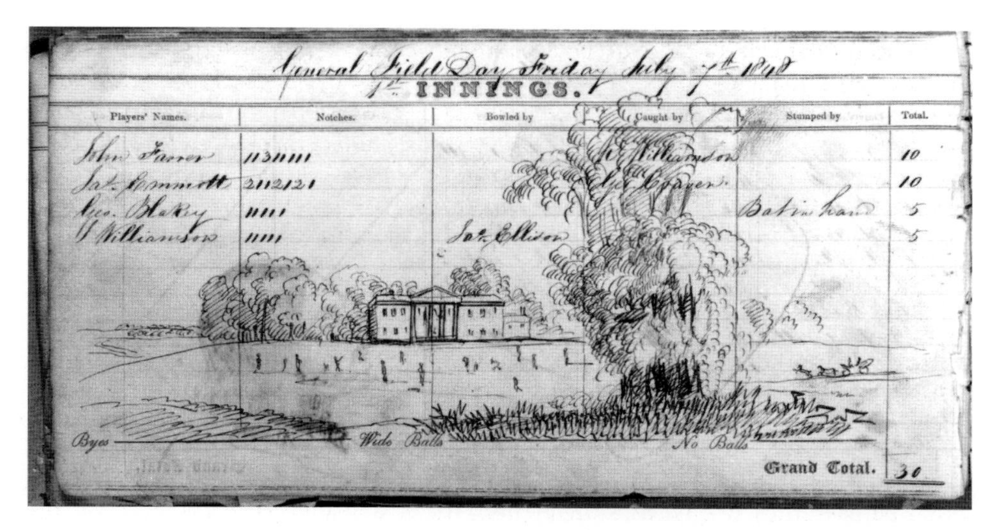

A page from the Keighley Cricket Club scorebook of 1848, showing a match in front of what appears to be Eastwood House.

First Prize of £6 at the Yorkshire Society's Meeting at Scarbro in 1847, and the First Prize of £10 at the Royal Agricultural Society of England Meeting at York in 1848'. Pig exhibitors at the Keighley Show were nicely divided into Gentlemen's, Farmers' and Labouring Men's classes.

A desire for home produce also led, in 1844, to the formation of a Land Society, under the secretaryship of another enterprising woolcomber, John Farrar Pickles. The then Rector, the Revd William Busfeild, was asked to 'use his influence' to get them a field to be divided into allotments; eleven spades, four forks, a shovel and 'the Privies belonging to Mittchil Mills in Coney Lane' were purchased; and a 'Gaffer' appointed to ensure that members fulfilled an obligation to work two days a week for the common good ('12 hours including meal times be caled one day'). Significantly, it was resolved 'that if any member be out of imployment he shall be imployed by the Society at the rate of 10 Shillings per week if convenient'. Minutes suggest that within a year they were growing corn and potatoes. In 1848 they were re-constituted the Keighley Allotment Society.

Sportsmen greeted the spring of 1848 by founding a Cricket Club, its select membership admitted by ballot, though there were less formal ways of acquiring players and equipment: 'Proposed by Isaac Sharpe, and seconded by Joseph Hardcastle, that a Cricket Ball, nearly new (submitted for inspection), from James Lund, be received into the Club as his subscription for the present year'. A 'bowling ground' down Dalton Lane was rented for £5 per annum, and after some weeks practising the team felt equal to playing a friendly Whit Monday game against Bingley (young Richard Hattersley, grandson of the founder machine-maker, was run out with a score of three). Thanks to a gifted doodler in the Club's original score-book, we learn that Keighley's first cricketers wore striped jerseys, retired into a tent with a flag on top when it rained, and occasionally played in the grounds of Eastwood House.

Towards mid-century, the physical town was taking on the shape by which it is still in part recognisable. The opening of the Market in 1833 moved five centuries of street trading out of Church Green. Street names – Brunswick, Adelaide, Hanover – suggest the period of their growth. Buildings were extending out along North Street: the Court House (1831), the Mechanics' Institute (1834). The post office transferred to more professional premises at the corner of College Street in 1839; and two years later the leisurely mail gig was superseded by a smart mail coach. William Robinson, Parish Church organist, scribbled an excited note of the scene: 'The first mail coach with four horses came into Keighley coachman and guard with scarlet coats the bells rung merrily and a band of music was engaged on the occasion'.

Indeed, by the late 1830s the traveller enjoyed a choice of coaches sporting brave names: from the Devonshire Arms ('there was always a crowd to see the coach,' one witness remembered) rattled the *Union* for Kendal and the *Invincible* for Preston ... from the King's Arms, the *Airedale*, Leeds-bound ... from the Fleece, the Leeds *Alexander*, the Bradford *Tradesman*, the Halifax *Wonder* ... carriers, too, were embarking on epic journeys to Kendal, Askrigg and Hawes. For several brief decades, roads rang to 'the merry clatter of the horses' feet and the stirring notes of the guard's key-bugle'; till the railways came to Keighley in 1847 in the shape of an extension of the Leeds and Bradford line, linked two years later with the East Lancashire through Colne to Manchester and Liverpool. To be sure, those first carriages were 'open trucks with seats round', but another era had arrived.

William White's West Riding Directory of 1847 reflects a busy town of many trades: seven wool comb makers, six reed and heald makers, nine manufacturers of rollers, spindles and flyers, six ironfounders, nine braziers, seven machine-makers, four nailmakers, five curriers, two dyers, five corn millers ... even the straw hat manufacturers had increased to twelve, and paper-making flourished at Morton, Ingrow and Goose Eye. There were six booksellers, seventeen private schools, a veterinary surgeon, Joseph Fawthrop (who kept a horse's skeleton in his North Street loft), and seven hairdressers, most of whom combined other businesses, Wilkinson Barwick also teaching music, Thomas Oldridge selling books, John Normington running a grocery shop. More specialised occupations included an umbrella maker, a tobacco pipe manufacturer, a 'bird stuffer' and a dealer in German clocks. Cotton spinning had almost disappeared by 1847, apart from Thomas Corlass in Hope and Cabbage Mills. Worsted spinners and manufacturers numbered thirty-four, who – the survivors out of sixty a decade earlier – were emerging as Keighley's household names, an industrial and social élite.

Their solid residences dominated the suburbs: the Sugdens at Eastwood House, the Briggs at Guard House, the Greenwoods at The Knowle, the Butterfields at

Chapter Four

Keighley's original railway station, built in 1847.

Cliffe House, the Haggases at Oakworth Hall, the Claphams at Aireworth House. Business connections were cemented by marriage: John Brigg – father of a more famous namesake who would become Knight and Member of Parliament – had married a Marriner, and one of his sons would marry another Marriner, and his daughter would marry a Craven. Mrs Brigg's mid-century letters chatter of family visits and holidays together: her son Willie sailing up the Rhine with 'the two Cravens from Steeton and William Clough and a gent from Bradford' … 'Miss Sugdens have left Eastwood House, they are staying at Cliffe at present' … 'Very little company in Harrogate. I expect my Hussey will want me to go with him, as he likes to be there, when Mr Craven is' … The important families brought a veneer of gracious living into a community which remained hugely rough and squalid.

Recitals of growing towns and developing trades can present an impression of general advancement and well-being, but for Keighley this would not be the complete picture: National problems of the age were reflected locally. For many – most, perhaps – life meant one continuous struggle against a grinding poverty. An inadequate diet, often devoid of meat and vegetables, led to what the Keighley Union surgeon graphically described as 'mental and physical depression, bloodless features, obstinate diarrhoea, and a sense of either sinking or falling away'. The staple porridge acquired an entire folklore, with tales like that of the old woman dying and asking for a last treat, who could imagine nothing grander than 'a toathree porridge with a little bit of butter in the middle': a state of affairs long blamed on the Corn Laws.

The most generally hated of a series of Corn Laws had, in 1815, increased the duties on imported grain, whilst granting freedom of export, thereby tending to keep home prices high. In 1826 (the year of the Butterworth Panic) the Keighley Select Vestry sent a petition to both Houses of Parliament, signed by 'upwards of two thousand' inhabitants who, 'in common with a majority of the People of England, are suffering severely from the decay of trade, which has been in a state of extreme depression for a great length of time. Under these circumstances they look forward to the meeting of Parliament with the most intense interest, because they believe that your honble. house has it in its power to afford material relief to the country, by removing those restrictions upon trade which the present corn Laws have imposed'. But not till 1846 were they repealed, a measure celebrated throughout the West Riding with the ringing of church bells and the firing of cannon. 'When we got the repeal of the Corn Laws,' a Keighley man would recall, 'my father bought some beef and other things, and he ordered my mother to make a good dinner; and when we sat down to it my mother stood over the table and cried, and said: "I have lived a long while in this world and never before saw a meal like this, nor never heard tell of such".'

Nevertheless, the 'hungry forties' did not improve overnight. This was the time of Chartism, of bitterness and unrest. In August of 1842 a mixed Lancashire and Yorkshire rabble rampaged through mill towns, knocking in the plugs of factory boilers and forcing work to a standstill. The Riot Act was read; troops doubled out of barracks; special constables were sworn in, shots exchanged in anger. At Keighley, a company of yeomanry reputedly distinguished themselves by galloping up to Lees Moor at news of a large crowd – to find only a congregation of Primitive Methodists holding a camp meeting! But authentically, the book-keeper at Calversyke Hill Mill recorded a three and a half days' closure with the single indignant word: 'Rioting'. Looking back at their Annual Meeting of August, 1843, the Improvement Commissioners regretted 'this time twelve months when the labouring population from a keen sense of suffering were aroused to acts of open insubordination, and the various Manufacturing establishments in this part of the Country were arrested by a lawless mob'; however, they were happy to report 'brighter and more cheering prospects'.

They spoke too soon. Within the week, woolcombers were placarding the town with a notice addressed to 'the Clergy, Gentry, Shopkeepers, and Inhabitants of Keighley Generally'. Eloquent of a period that remains indifferently documented, this is worth quoting at some length:

> We, the WOOLCOMBERS of KEIGHLEY and Vicinity, take the liberty of presenting the following facts to your notice, in the full confidence of your sympathy and support. You may perhaps be generally aware that our condition, as a body of working men,

> has been anything but prosperous for a considerable time back. Through the frequent reductions in our wages, and alterations in the wool, an excellent Comber has been only able to earn, on an average, about Eight or Nine Shillings per week when in full employment. As might naturally be supposed, since the late improvement in trade a wish has been manifested on our part, to raise the price of our labour some little, knowing, that unless we did so, the first depression again in trade would probably sink us lower than ever. On stating our wish to some of the Manufacturers, one very Influential Firm, viz. MESSRS. MARRINER, agreed to our request in a very gentlemanly manner. Having so far succeeded, we thought it only reasonable to cause the advance to become general, and for that purpose we agreed to draw out the Men in the employ of MESSRS. LUND, WHITEHEAD, & WILLIAMSON, intending, as they were only amongst the smallest Firms in the Town, to support the Men ourselves during the strike, and thus avoid becoming burthensome to the Public. Judge, however, of our surprise, when, to frustrate our intention, the bulk of the Manufacturers left word this Morning, before setting off to Bradford Market, that unless we resumed our work to-day, and gave up all attempts at an advance they would every one cease weighing out Wool to-morrow morning, and thus put an end to the strike by a general stoppage...

Seen in this context, woolcomber John Farrar Pickles's Land Society of 1844, with its members gardening two twelve-hour days a week and its provision for those unemployed, suggests an atmosphere of short time and industrial laying off of workers.

In 1846 a Protective Society of the Power-Loom Weavers of Keighley and Neighbourhood was established, membership a penny a week for weavers and a halfpenny for winders and spinners. Ideally, its object was 'the cultivation of a good understanding and a friendly intercourse between the employer and employed'. Its Committee stressed 'that we have no wish to enter into a warfare with honourable employers who are disposed to act with justice and reason towards us'; but they were authorised 'to lay levies of so much per Member, for the purpose of obtaining an advance of wages, or resisting a reduction'.

The sequel is best told in the words of a neutral spectator. 'We have here,' a Keighley nurseryman wrote that October to his daughter away from home, 'a most extensive and determined contest between the Wool Combers and their masters which has now lasted eight weeks every master in the Town except three dismissed their men in order to prevent them from supporting the men belonging to one master who were on strike for a very small advance which these Free Traders had promised them' – this hints at an over-optimism following the abolition of the Corn Laws – 'there was one Thousand five Hundred combers out of work in Keighley some have got employment elsewhere many are thrown on the Parish which makes the poor rates very heavy, and it is only two or three months since there was a strike amongst the poor [power] Loom weavers when many hundreds chiefly women were out for some time'. Complained a Grassington manufacturer to Robert Clough, at whose mill the trouble had started: 'I really dare not come into Keighley with my cart until this excitement is over'.

An Exley Head letter-writer, in October, 1853, summarises the results of a decade of strikes and turn-outs: 'flower is dear £1. 10s. per pack potatoes ditto. the trade is worse for weavers and combers they are lowering wages and many out of work'. By then, many of Keighley's woolcombers lived 'in the depths of extreme poverty, rarely tasting animal food from year to year', and a survey was made as to their wages and diet. John Lilly's family of eight (he earned 7s 6d a week: rent 1s 6d) ate 'no meat, but a sheep's head occasionally'; Joseph Maude, with a family of five, had 'not 2s. worth for the last 12 months'; and some, like J. Sunderland who kept five dependents (one was working for 2s a week) on less than a shilling a day, simply never ate meat, 'unless ordered by the Union surgeon in case of sickness'.

Chapter Five

Mid-century Keighley – immigration and emigration – Babbage and Ranger Reports

In 1845, 1846 and 1847 the Irish potato crop failed and led to a massive emigration. The daughter of John Butterfield, a Keighley timber merchant, would remember her father 'helping to find accommodation for Irish brought over during the Potato Famine': suddenly the town was filling with Kellys and Flynns, Mahoneys and Durkins and Gallaghers, O'Haras and Walshes. Typhus fever wrought havoc amongst them, despite the Board of Guardians' providing 'a very liberal allowance of wine, brandy, and other stimulants'; yet by 1851 – after a decade in which the population rushed from 13,378 to 18,258 – one person in twenty in Keighley was Irish.

The more resilient, with an eagle eye for opportunity, had set up as lodging-house keepers; the worsted mills employed their women and children; men worked as agricultural, masons' and railway labourers, or as excavators. An inordinate number were hawkers, of pots, baskets, hardware; several were journeyman tailors. One Thaddeus Faughy described himself as a musician. A local versifier contrived a lucid picture of another popular 'modus operandi':

The Irish pedlars who parade our streets,
For rags and bones give children sweets:
Old hoofs and horns, old nails and rabbit-skins,
Old gloves, old hats, and used-up tins,
All's treasured up — there's nothing comes amiss;
His pack in swelling, swells his soul with bliss.
Blythly he bears the load and wends his way,
When lengthening shadows mark the close of day.
At night he sorts the varied goods he's got,
And piles up each into a separate lot;
Then on the morn with glee the lots he takes
And of the whole a goodly sum he makes...

Nineteenth-century living conditions: Westgate, with a gathering of children.

The Irish settled, according to the nature of immigrants, in specific quarters; and, since they had left conditions of the most squalid poverty, they gravitated precisely towards those crowded streets which were already fast deteriorating into slums: Damside and the Pinfold, the Ginnel and Baptist Square. redolent with swill-tubs and ash-places; Carrodus Square at Upper Green, with its open drain; out along South Street to Nelson Street ('filthy open drains'), the King Street Club-Houses ('open cesspool to privy, very full'), and the evil Brickhouses where families huddled into cellars. Some fifty congregated up Fell Lane ('filthy open drain from top to bottom'); and another fifty at Goose Eye, the majority finding work as rag-cutters in the paper mill.

Indeed, by mid-century Keighley's population growth had outstripped the adequacies of its sewerage, drainage, sanitation and water supply. Standing puddles 'of foul and offensive liquid matter' seeped through walls and into cellars. The North Beck, flowing through packed homes, was, to put it mildly, polluted. Fresh water was generally lacking. Unventilated back-to-back houses reeked with bad air. Disgusting privies and soil-pits, pig-sties and heaps of manure, stank in yards and snickets – in one instance, a single privy was shared by twenty houses; in others, the ratio was three to sixty-six, and six to ninety. Pig-owners made a depressing practice of slaughtering their produce on their door-steps in the small hours; poultry ran about constantly underfoot; people habitually emptied 'chamber utensils in front of houses in broad day'.

In Leeds Street, strewn with 'ashes and other refuse, filthy and nauseous', somebody was boiling 'bellies and other animal matter for pigs in a room under a dwelling-house'; the adjoining pigsty was predictably 'very filthy'. Eastwood Square presented 'filthy open drains, large accumulations of ashes and garbage and swill-tubs, also a most filthy and offensive privy-pit, at the bottom, quite full of ashes, and the place completely covered with the excrements of children'. In Mill Hill, a tank filled with the contents of residents' privy, slops and eaves, then ran through a wall into the road to the Beck. A board privy at the top of Knowle Lane seemed 'scarcely sufficient to cover any one from view'; whilst a urinal in New Bridge Street was 'very wet and filthy'. Privy refuse crawled down cellar bedroom walls in King Street and Nelson Street. Strong Close Lane was 'almost impassable from excrement'.

Of course, death and disease stalked such wretched dwellings. When dreaded cholera threatened, the town was placarded with recommendations: 'Where offensive exhalations arise, they should be destroyed by the Solution of Chloride of Lime'. It was necessary to advise people to change their clothes from time to time, and – 'if available' – indulge in 'occasional warm bathing'. Mercifully, cholera spared Keighley, but other ailments did not. Smallpox, dysentery, scarlatina and measles exacted their toll; whooping cough, croup, influenza, diarrhoea, typhus and rheumatic fever killed; scores wilted and died of consumption, asthma, paralysis ... nearly half the fatalities were under five years old. At Haworth, an average life expectancy was 25.8 years, and forty-one per cent of deaths were of children less than six years old. Rebecca Town, a Keighley woman who died in 1851 in her forty-fourth year, achieved a pathetic notoriety by having borne thirty children who all died in their infancy.

Human detail, seldom apparent in statistics, is poignantly supplied by the surviving letters of such townsfolk as were literate. 'The Dear little creature does not appear to suffer any pain,' wrote the outfaced grandfather of a baby whose mother had just died, 'but takes his pap and sleeps very well but it grieves us much to see him gradually growing less and thiner every day in spite of all we can doo for him ... P.S. he has been loose in his bowels for two or three days, indeed he has been generally so since we had him which will of cours weaken him much'. Again: 'You must come soon if you see her alive,' an Exley Head farmer writes of his nephew's young wife 'sinking rapidly in Consumtion' and leaving another motherless baby, 'we think she will not continue long she has had a great desire to get better but her nurs has tould her she niver will get better Mr Mayne [the Ingrow vicar] visits her but she can only wisper now her cough is Bad but she doth not complain...'

'I do not know whether you would like at Keighley,' one man cautioned a friend who contemplated removing in 1853, 'it is a poor place'. Provisions were dear: 'potatoes 1s. 2d. – 16 lb flower 3s. 8d. Meal 4s. 4d. – 28 lb Butter 13½d – 16 oz Milk 1½d. per quart Eggs 16 for 1s.' The Poor Rates grew so heavy that one Guardian opined, in 1855, that they should 'relieve no able-bodied young men, as there was plenty of work for them in the Crimea'. At the next Board elections, his political opposition refuted him through the not uncommon medium of a poster addressed 'To the Inhabitants of the Keighley Union':

> You will all understand that this means, neither more nor less than that any young man, so unfortunate as to be out of work, is either to die at home of hunger, or run the immediate hazard of a violent and bloody death on the field of Battle, for a Shilling a day, for a system that denies him a home and a Living in his own country.

This same placard divulged that a Guardian had technically abused his office by 'keeping Three Cochin China Hens, at the Keighley Workhouse a few days to keep them from the dirt and smoke of the town, previous to their exhibition at a Poultry Show'; and, more seriously, offers an entire sinister dimension on the troubled relations between masters and men, by alleging that workhouse inmates 'may be drafted from there to the factory, farm, and workshop, on the terms agreed upon by the employer and the Board, to assist in reducing the wages of other operatives'. Philanthropic bodies struggled to supplement the cold charity of overworked official relief: during 1856 the Wesleyan Dorcas Society gave away 32 handkerchiefs, 36 aprons, 69 petticoats, 27 singlets, 54 shirts, 139 chemises, eighteen sheets and four pinafores.

Some sought escape in emigration: 'Wm. Corlass is gone to Austrilia and left his wife and famly' ... 'Leach and famly are gon into amirica'. One Keighley widow, Mrs Smith, who sailed to the Cape of Good Hope in 1848, left a journal of her 71-day voyage beset by gales, a collision, suspected smallpox and 'a disturbance between Capt. & Crew'; naturally she longed for her 'own quiet home again'. By the 1850s, B.W. Barwick's Market music-shop was doubling as booking agency for the Australian Black Ball Line; china dealer Nathan Aldersley of North Street issued tickets for Eagle Line clippers; whilst John Farrar Pickles, now set up as a supplier of funeral biscuits and 'temperance cordials', offered weekly sailings for those 'intending to emigrate to America, Australia, or any of the British Colonies'. Even the penniless could get abroad, for a consideration: 'Wanted Immediately,' stressed an advertisement of 1855, 'a Woolsorter, (Single Man,) to go out to the Cape of Good Hope. Constant Employment will be given'. (The following year, one Mary Ann Peel and her three children were destitute; the reason: 'Husband gone to Cape of Good Hope'.)

As some left, others came – Keighley's position attracted 'the scum of the great stream of migration between Carlisle, the North. Liverpool, Ireland and America, Manchester and the upper parts of Lancashire, in the one direction; and Bradford, Leeds, Wakefield, the great manufacturing towns of the West Riding, and all the

SOUTH AFRICA.

WANTED

IMMEDIATELY

A WOOLSORTER,

(SINGLE MAN,)

To go out to the Cape of Good Hope.

Constant Employment will be given.

Apply to JOHN HOLMES, Grocer.

J. L. CRABTREE, PRINTER & STATIONER, CHANGE-GATE, KEIGHLEY

A local emigration poster of 1855.

Midlands, in the other.' This statement, of 1866, is only a partial exaggeration. The 1841 census had revealed a little community of thirty-three nomadic souls, the families of four earthenware dealers, a broom-maker and a razor-grinder, squatting in tents at Utley Green Head. A decade and more later the vagrant trickle had become a flood.

Keighley, it was fervidly claimed, was 'the grand depot for the wholesale importation' of beggars, prostitutes and petty criminals; tramps approaching the workhouse casual wards were known to burn their clothes so as to qualify for fresh ones. But the bulk of this floating population found accommodation – such as it was – in the town's lodging-houses, where beds were let out at threepence a night, 'and it frequently happens that the man or woman taking a single bed, sublets it to four or five more'. John Milligan, the Union surgeon, said he had entered rooms where vermin would 'drop on my hat from the ceiling like peas'; when he visited lodging-houses, he used to wear black trousers, 'in order that I may see the lice which get on them, to remove them'.

A survey of such haunts resembled, predictably but aptly, a descent into Dante's underworld. One Keighley doss-house was 'nothing but a common brothel, frequented by none but prostitutes and thieves'. In another – not named at the time but almost certainly the Brickhouses — dozens of men and women crowded together on a cellar floor, alternately sleeping and copulating. Upstairs, partitioned into cubicles, beds were 'black and filthy, and in some cases wet'; after each being crammed with half-a-dozen men and women every night, the stench was 'abominable'. In the attic 'lay an elderly strumpet, beastly drunk, her hair dishevelled, her face battered, and the blood flowing out of the corner of her mouth'. At a third house, investigators surprised a seventy-year-old man 'in bed with a woman of three or four-and-twenty, who saluted the intruders with bawdy "chaff"'; whilst in the next room the keeper, in his sixties 'and married', had intercourse with a teenage girl (whose mother sat meanwhile behind a rag curtain).

Nothing evokes this seamy mid-century life more graphically than a diary kept, between 1848 and 1853, by James Leach, one of the six watchmen who, by then, were patrolling the streets for 16s 6d a week, 'with the use of coats, caps, oil, and lamps'. Public houses provided a ready escape from squalor (White's 1853 Directory lists twenty-four inns and twenty-two beershops in Keighley); the licensing laws were slack ('compny at Thomas Blakey Beear Shop all night till 5 Clock on Friday Morning'): and nightly unfortunates were borne to the 'lock up' lapsed into varying degrees of 'rather refreshed', 'part drunk', 'drunk', 'drunk and disordley', 'drunk and very disordley', 'fast asleep' – the latter retrieved from ginnels and doorsteps, carts and market-stalls, pig-sties and gravestones. A cow doctor was picked up dead drunk under his horse's belly at Eastwood Row; one Joseph Tyas outside the Mechanics' Institute early on a January morning, 'and the hair of is head frosen to the ground'. Leach's diary chronicles a common background of free fights and what were quaintly termed 'Irish rows' ('the Lanlord at Wool Pack inn and William Holt striped stark naked in the street fiting and100 persons round them' ... 'whe was sent for to Abrham shakeltons the Lord Rodney inn to quash a disturbance betwixt him and his wife and hir Childrin. Abrham got too black eyes and altogether it was a very ruf house'); prostitution ('2 females in Morleys pasage disordley with 5 or 6 Irish men' .... 'Cathrinah Sulivan strouling the streets with 15 men'); and notorious riff-raff like Samuel Smith 'comonley caled Mucky Sam' who 'threw Patrick Waterhouse over the batlment at Damside a depth of 5 yards & cut & wounded im daingerousley'.

Crime filtered upwards from the bottom of this brutalised community. There was a good deal of senseless or malicious vandalism, such as the killing of sheep, the cutting off of cows' tails, and the sabotaging of building works. Suicide was far from rare: one relieving officer gave himself a fatal dose of laudanum; another (Abraham Wildman) had a nervous breakdown. A workhouse master was controversially acquitted of having poisoned his wife.

The locality's murders, by and large, were of an apparently motiveless, irrational nature now regarded as symptomatic of societies turned sick and desperate. In 1839, a young shoemaker in the King Street Club-Houses cut his sister's throat, 'and if I had not done so,' he confessed, 'there would have been great commotions in the

Febry 8 ½p12 Clock on Sunday Morning
a prostetute the name
of Clanker in the
Market place and
Several men about hir
Ordred hir of home

12 ½p12 Clock on Thursday Morning
James Marran drunk
and Kicking up a great
disturbance in the
Babtist Squair,

25 ½p3 Clock on Wedensday
Morning 2 Straingers found
in Mr Mitchell Boiler
house who aquainted the
Master and he let
them of

29 ½p12 Clock on Sunday Morning
a Irish row at the
dam Side James Smith
and Several more

A page from James Leach's diary for 1852, booking, among others, 'a prostetute the name of Clanker'.

land, great winds, rains, flood, and Butterfield's Factory pulled down'. In 1861, the keeper of the Hawkcliffe toll-bar shot his wife and wounded his brother-in-law: 'I can't remember aught about it,' he apologised, 'I have been very bad in my head'. In 1864, a tenant at Greenhouse Farm, Guard House, beat in his wife's head with a spade. He had been 'in a somewhat low and desponding state of mind' for months, and was heard to remark when appearing before the magistrates: 'What have they brought me here for? I have done nowt'. This case caused a sensation because the murderer hid for a night and a day up the Lower Holme Mills goit, and subsequently hanged himself with his garters in his cell at York Castle.

Poverty and squalor were not confined to the town centre. A walk out of Haworth by way of Enfield Side and beyond the Lumb Beck waterfall, in the highly romanticised Brontë era, would have followed, not today's empty moors, but a succession of small, struggling grey farms – Bottoms, Hill End, Virginia. Dean Side, Forks House, Lower Withens – some of whose occupants were scratching as little as three acres. Of necessity. they supplemented their existence by woolcombing or handloom weaving, or by working in mills and quarries. One nameless derelict, known only as Lucky Luke, dragged out for twenty years a wretched life against the idyllic background of Holme House Wood, his iron-grey beard hanging down to his waist, rags tied to his legs and body with rope. 'I herd him tell my mother who was a kind harted warken woman,' a neighbourhood boy recalled, 'that he had often Changed Clothing with the scarecrows and Some times for months together he would never be sene by mortel man unless with Such as my Self who invaded his Solitude allthough gardens or turnup feald often ware Plundered'.

The Riddlesden and Morton Banks landscape was scarred – till 1856 – with coal workings, a complex of shallow shafts or 'day-holes' abandoned when they ran too deep for convenience. The seam was six feet thick in places, but water-logged, and the coal of inferior quality. 'The cinder and ash that remain after combustion,' one manufacturer wrote, 'are almost, if not quite, equal to the unburnt coal in bulk'. There were further pits at Parkwood (a contemporary speaks of seeing 'women as well as men' working in them), but an undated plan of the Keighley Colliery is repeatedly marked 'Bad Coal' and 'This part full of water'.

Hard life, however, enjoyed refuges other than drink and debauchery. Religious appeal was simple and straightforward, the hymns of the day pleasantly distinguished by localised tunes like 'Moorcock', 'Simmerstone', 'Daisy Hill'. Many industrialists took a genuine paternal interest in the spiritual wellbeing of their labouring classes: the Greenwood family boasted a lengthy record of benefactions to the Parish Church; the Briggs became synonymous with the growth of Keighley Congregationalism. Jonas Sugden and Brothers, staunch Methodists of Vale Mill, Oakworth, issued a series of regulations beginning, first: 'We wish and expect that every person in our employ attend some place of Divine Worship every Lord's Day'; and second: 'That every youth, dependent upon those whom we employ, attend some Sunday and Day School, from the age of six years and upwards'. Their workers were compulsorily enrolled in the Vale Mill Sick Club, and received no benefits during disability 'brought on by any immoral conduct'. If such edicts appear overbearing to modern eyes, they form a welcome contrast to more normal factory rules primarily concerned with fining late-comers and punishing negligence.

Church and chapel were acquiring, too, an increasing importance in Victorian social life. A Sunday School Committee minute-book from Hall Green Baptist Chapel, Haworth, records with simple eloquence the weeks of preparation culminating in annual Whit Monday festivities: Resolved 'that John Townend shall ask a few musicians to play on Whit Monday' ... 'that 360 Cakes be made at 2d. each & that Betty Hartley & Mary Hudson be requested to make them' ... 'that 2 Strikes of Malts & 8 oz. of Hops be bought of Tobias Lambert & that Mary Wright be engaged to brew it & to make 7 or 8 Gallons of beer' ... 'that we invite the Horkin scholars & Teachers to visit us on that occasion & if so disposed, that the Hall Green scholars meet them on the New Road' ... 'that Mr Winterbotham's scholars join the Hall Green scholars near West Lane chapel and they walk down Haworth together'.... But here again, the inevitable sadness: children absent from Sunday School because they were too cold, because they had 'no clothes', because they were sick.

If the middle years of the nineteenth century represent Keighley's nadir, help was even then at hand. In 1848, stirred by the national ravages of cholera, the Public Health Act advocated a course of sanitary reform by means of a central authority empowered to set up Local Boards of Health. Hereabouts, Haworth showed the way; on October 9th, 1849, some 222 residents, concerned at their lack of 'a sufficient supply of pure and wholesome water', petitioned the General Board of Health 'to direct a Superintending Inspector to visit the said chapelry or district, and to make inquiry and examination with respect thereto, with a view to the application of the said Act'.

The following spring, Benjamin Herschel Babbage spent three penetrating days at Haworth, then a bustling little town of some two and a half thousand inhabitants listing, besides its staple population of farmers, woolcombers and stone masons, six cloggers and eleven boot and shoe-makers, eight tailors and seven cabinet-makers, two doctors, two booksellers, the grammar school and two 'academies', several worsted mills, a temperance hotel, and a tinner and brazier who also kept the post office. Four carriers provided a measure of public transport, and an omnibus went to Bradford and Halifax on market days, and 'to meet trains at Keighley'. To be sure, the Superintending Inspector's first impressions recall *Wuthering Heights*: 'The face of the country around Haworth is very hilly and bleak, as there are but few trees to arrest the wintry winds'; thereafter he reverted to hard prose.

He found woolcombers working in their own bedrooms, maintaining the necessary high temperature by burning stoves day and night and never opening windows. In a cellar-dwelling, a family of seven slept in two beds in their combing-shop. He counted privies – sixty-nine to all Haworth. Twenty-four houses in the main street shared a single privy; another seven had none at all. One, used by a dozen families, 'perched upon an eminence, commanding the whole length of the main street', above an overflowing cesspit. Haworth had no sewers, only a few covered drains, and most refuse ran along open gutters. He perambulated fifty midden-steads and twenty-three manure heaps. One at West Lane, next to a row of back-to-back cottages, was piled with entrails, slaughterhouse garbage, and what was graphically described as 'green meat' thrown out of a butcher's. He noted 'the most crying want' of water. There were eleven pumps (including two that were out of order), but few used them for cooking, 'as they do not fancy that this water is pure'; the more fastidious would walk up to half a mile for water from the Head Well, which nonetheless in summer grew 'so green and putrid' that cattle refused to drink it. An enterprising Mr Thomas had built a cistern at Sowden's Spring, and leakily piped water to thirty or forty houses. One tap was within two yards of the cesspit in the main street. The graveyard, less than an acre in extent, had received 1,344 burials during the previous ten years, accumulating 'too great a collection in one place of decomposing matter'.

Not surprisingly, Superintending Inspector Babbage recommended 'the application of the Public Health Act' – that is, the election of a Local Board of Health – 'to the hamlet of Haworth and the parts adjacent'. Such was the urgency of the situation that although the state of Oxenhope and Stanbury was similarly 'very bad' (they were subject to typhus fever), he rejected their inclusion in immediate measures 'as it might lead to delay in the application of the Act to Haworth'.

Keighley followed suit early in 1854, when 472 residents petitioned the General Board of Health for an inquiry – 270 of these, it transpired, had signed on the misunderstanding 'that the party soliciting signatures were merely seeking a reduction of the water-rate', and asked to be cancelled! Superintending Inspector William Ranger visited the town notwithstanding, that same autumn, his squalid findings rivalling those of his colleague at Haworth. Three decades of over-population had long outgrown the provisions of the Waterworks and Improvement Acts. He could commend the Commissioners on their gas-lighting ('and the accounts are admirably kept') and night-watching, but otherwise Keighley represented the familiar pattern of omissions and inadequacies. Sewage disposal was non-existent. Drainage and sanitation were glaringly deficient. There were no proper regulations governing paving and the removal of nuisances. Mr Ranger had poked his discerning nose into more than 170 yards and entries, yet found only three privies consistent with 'the rules of decency'. He recommended the setting up of a Local Board of Health.

About the time of the inquiry, the Improvement Commissioners significantly concerned themselves about 'the propriety of refraining from throwing any more Ashes into the Beck or Watercourse adjoining the Gas yard', and after a month's deliberation resolved to stop dumping, not only ashes, but also 'Liquor, Tar or any rubbish or thing whatsoever' ('until further orders'). Early the next year they moved 'that the establishment of the Public Health Act in this Town as recommended by the Report of Mr Ranger be opposed by the Commissioners'; but, well-meaning men insufficiently primed, they were too late. On August 31st,

Chapter Five

Early housing at its worst: the smallest house in Keighley, photographed at Damside in 1924.

1855, they met 'to take into consideration the application of the Public Health Act 1848 to this district'. Three weeks later Keighley's affairs passed under the authority of a Local Board.

It was not a particularly grand occasion. The retiring Commissioners had little to hand over except the gasworks and a £6,000 debt. Some difficulty was experienced in persuading eligible candidates – they had to be payers of at least £10 a year in poor-rates – to stand for election to the twenty-one-strong Board; though according to one observer 'the new Act appears to be very popular amongst the working classes'. Indeed, a more radical element placarded the town with slogans ('Monopoly is blown up! Self-election is set aside! Family rule has come to an end! Autocracy has been exchanged for Democracy!') and nominated twenty-one candidates pledged 'to equalize and lessen the price of gas, to increase the supply and cheapen the price of water, to see that the houses of the poor are as well watched as the mills and mansions of the rich, to protect the footway of the working-man as sacredly as the carriage-way of the squire, to prevent the work of the town being done by strangers while residents of sufficient ability may be found, and in no case to extort payment for that which has not been supplied'. Eight of these were successful.

In the event, the twenty-one members first elected to Keighley's Local Board of Health included only five who had previously served as Improvement Commissioners: four manufacturers, Joseph Craven (the Chairman), John Clough, William Lund and B. Flesher Marriner, together with reed maker Joseph Smith; though additionally manufacturer Isaac Hird, stuff piece maker Henry Rishworth, and toolmaker William Smith were entering public life. The rest comprised three farmers, two drapers, a butcher, a hatter and a tea merchant, the Registrar and a book-keeper, an innkeeper, a spinner and a corn miller.

Responsibility was shifting its emphasis from the manufacturers towards the smaller tradesmen – men, as an election poster had idealistically put it, 'with clear heads, large hearts, and clean hands'.

Chapter Six

Local Board of Health – newspapers and periodicals– Spiritualism – Co-operative Society – Rifle Volunteers – Waterworks – railways – gasworks – baths and wash-houses – Anti-Vaccinationists

The Keighley Local Board of Health would hold sway for twenty-seven years and lay the foundations of the town's local government for most of the century after that, but of course nothing was done overnight; in fact, for some months nothing – beyond gasworks routine – was done at all. Then in 1856 the Board published its bye-laws.

These formulated a businesslike code of conduct for regular meetings and the appointment of sub-committees: soon after its inception the Board had formed a Finance Committee and another for Lighting and Watching, which met weekly or fortnightly. Their Clerk — solicitor William Burr — attended to their paperwork and advised on legal matters. Other officers were a combined Surveyor and Inspector of Nuisances, a Superintendent of the Gas Works, a Rate Collector, and a Superintendent of Police.

The latter euphemistic post was filled by the chief watchman, a former Bradford police sergeant, who was given an ideal set of instructions but little else: 'He shall be held responsible for the peace of the district, and for the lives and the property therein' ... 'He must ascertain, as far as possible, that all his men are physically fit for their work, that they are clean and neat in their persons, that they are strictly sober, that they are cool and cautious, that they are firm – yet good-tempered, courteous and obliging – that they are creditably intelligent and virtuous' ... 'He shall vigorously enforce the performance of all the men's duties; and for this purpose he must be constantly passing to and fro among them – imparting directions, instruction, and encouragement'. However, the inauguration of the West Riding Constabulary at the beginning of 1857 transferred police duties into the understandably more capable hands of a regular force.

The Inspector of Nuisances, too, enjoyed a comprehensive if still partly theoretical authority. He was responsible for street-cleansing and scavenging, for the periodic inspection of graveyards, lodging-houses, cellar-dwellings, butcher-shops and slaughter-houses. He was enjoined to maintain a strict vigilance on ponds and drains, privies and dung-heaps, and prosecute any waste or fouling of water, or 'any case of swine kept in a dwelling-house'.

The Local Board of Health bye-laws extended and particularised some of the clauses of the 1824 Improvement Act, retaining their general cautions against 'furiously' riding or driving horses, obstructing pavements, breaking lamps or throwing fireworks. Now, however, builders were to submit plans showing 'the situation and construction of the privies and cesspools to be built'; dwellings could be compulsorily whitewashed and their owners sued for neglect. There were stipulations as to the minimum width of new streets and thoroughfares. Slaughter-houses were to be 'thoroughly whitewashed with quick lime' every March and September, unsound meat confiscated and its vendors fined. Publicans countenancing 'common prostitutes, reputed thieves, or idle or disorderly persons' on their premises were liable to prosecution. Lodging-houses were to be registered annually, open for inspection, and 'the number and size of the beds' regulated 'for better securing cleanliness, good order, and morality'; blankets to be cleaned 'at least' four times a year.

Such considerations may not of themselves appear spectacular, but civilisations stand or fall by them. Demonstrably, too, a yawning gulf separates the framing of rules from their translation into reality; yet now at least the approximately literate public had an object through which to air their requests, complaints, advice and views. Letters began to pour in to the offices — first in New Bridge Street, later in Devonshire Street — of the Keighley Board of Health:

> Sirs, Will you be so kind as to send for me to relate to you some information respecting to a Shop front that Mr Steel occupies in Low Street he frequently puts goods on it and it belongs to the town the local bord ad to pull the railing down some time since and i think it aught to be kept Clear. Also he as a grate fild up wich aught to be opned as he has a water Closet in the house on the ground floor and not being opned he is smelled out with is own stink … I beg to call your attention to Park Lane and request you, to have the road repaired … There is an open drain alongside the footpath in Spring Gardens, and in order to cross the road to my door it is necessary to stride across it a distance of from two to three feet ... 'Please put us a crossing into our land adjoining Skipton Road and charge us with the cost ... Will you kindly oblige by looking & enquiring into the Matter of a Drain that requires altering in Adelaide Street. So long as it remains in the state it is very bad smells arise from it, and I am anxious that it should be looked to & altered before the warm weather setts in … As the children, my wife and some friends were going to the Tarn on Thursday, the Stink from Mr Walbank's dead horse boiling place was so sickening that they had to put their handkerchiefs over their mouths and noses and rush past till they got to the other side of the building…

Chapter Six

Church Green, about the 1860s. The cameraman's roof-top activities have brought the whole street out to look.

Actually, the town's shortcomings were no worse than typical of their period and circumstances: the Rivers Commission, lengthily reporting on the state of the Aire and its tributaries in 1867, painted a dark canvas of its entire course 'abused, obstructed and polluted to an extent scarcely conceivable by other than eye-witnesses'. At Keighley an accumulation of rubbish was thought to have raised the beds of the Worth and the North Beck by four or five feet over the past thirty-five years, with resultant stopping of mill-wheels, blocking of drains and flooding of cellars. Machine-maker Richard Longden Hattersley described how his firm habitually dumped their refuse: 'Our place is a very awkward place, and we have to lead the ashes to the land if we cart them away, therefore it is a great convenience to us to be able to put them into the beck'. Another Commission witness cast his mind back three decades to remember a rustic scene of 'trout coming up to spawn and jumping the dam stones five or six feet, to get higher up into the river, where there were sandy beds in which they could deposit their spawn'; woolcombers used to come 'to capture trout at the dam stones'. Naturally, there were no trout by 1867.

Even by 1861, nevertheless, White's Directory felt able to compliment the Local Board on Keighley's 'greatly improved' sanitary condition. Its early members were grappling with divers other problems, replacing street name-boards, vainly attempting smoke control, putting up decorations for the Agricultural Show, fencing dangerous quarries. One lengthy serio-comedy of 1864 centred on a shafting which Messrs Hattersley had erected across Water Lane – when the Board sent men forcibly to cut down this obstruction, Hattersleys' workers attacked them with 'red-hot iron bars'. Another arose over the Board's relations with the press.

For the community was developing in many directions now, and there were local papers. The Temperance Society pioneered the way with a free monthly called *The Keighley Visitor* which first came out in October, 1853, and which, subsequently priced at a halfpenny and then at a penny, would continue till the end of 1872. The *Visitor*, whilst largely composed of moral essays and propaganda, is occasionally illuminating: 'Ellis Hartley, of Haworth, fined 5s. and costs, for being drunk, or to sit six hours in the stocks' … 'Joseph Spence, alias "Boxer", was placed in the stocks, Church Green, for gambling, at the beginning of March, in a lane near Exley Head. A crowd of people witnessed his punishment'. Incidentally, Keighley's powerful Temperance Society of the era campaigned successfully for the removal of the stocks from Church Green. The site was occupied by a drinking fountain presented to the town in 1869 by Miss Butterfield of Cliffe Hall, which hopefully 'would no doubt be of greater service to the public' – though offenders unable to pay fines, now deprived of the option of brazening out a few hours in the stocks, were sentenced instead to lengthier spells in Wakefield House of Correction.

In April, 1854, appeared a monthly with a cumbersome title angling for a wide sales area, *The Keighley and Haworth Argus, and Kildwick, Cross Hills, Steeton, and Silsden Advertiser.* This, as the *Visitor* was quick to point out, was little more than 'a London Illustrated Paper, sent down here with two or three blank pages, to suit the requirements of the Keighley editor' — one T.D. Hudson, of the High Street — which survived for sixteen months. This same Hudson, in 1855, attempted the town's first weekly newspaper, the *Keighley News and Airedale Advertiser*, which ran for possibly just four issues. After Hudson's failure, J. Harrison & Son, the Bingley printers, added *The Keighley Advertiser* to the title of their *Airedale Courant*, continuing thus till 1858 but chiefly made up in London. J.M. Jowett, proprietor of *The Bradford Advertiser*, published a local edition called *The Keighley and Skipton Mercury* in 1856 and 1857; this was a Liberal weekly upholding 'progress without anarchy, order without despotism', but, again, emanated from London; as did Robert Aked's *Illustrated Monthly Journal and Keighley Advertiser* of 1858, and *The Keighley Guardian* of 1860. A more independent but short-lived *Keighley Monthly Recorder,* early in 1860, was 'conducted by a number of working men denominated a Local Affairs Committee', whose first issue, the rival *Visitor* tartly observed, was 'entirely occupied with an address to the Readers, a report of the meeting of the board of health, and a railway time table'.

The years have not been kind to these mid-century publications, of which, in several cases, no known copies exist. Modest though they were, their few pages of local announcements and advertisements are eloquent of their period. Editors had an endearing habit of filling out their columns with snippets like 'How to Kill Bugs and Other Vermin' ('Rats and mice speedily disappear by mixing equal quantities of strong cheese and powdered squills') and 'How to Keep a Pig for Sixpence a Week' ('Take ¼lb. of Irish moss, 3lbs of Indian meal, boil in 16 gallons of water, this makes 16 gallons of very strong jelly, and will keep a large pig one week at a cost of sixpence').

Trades and professions are glimpsed through their advertising. The Grammar School has engaged a French master, Monsieur Mercier, and advises parents not to allow their offspring 'to mix with loose companions in the streets'; Mr Cockroft prepares students for 'any commercial situation, or appointment in the Civil Service'; whilst your children can enjoy full board and a comprehensive education at Crowle's Classical, Mathematical, and Commercial Academy for £24 per annum (washing £2 extra). J. Naylor of Corn Mill Bridge is scaling, filling and 'carefully' extracting teeth in between selling cigars and snuff; Mrs Hanson boasts a stock of fresh leeches; photographer G. Morton 'has erected a Gallery for the purpose of producing Portraits on the most modern and approved scientific principles of the art'. Joseph Clapham extols his Noted Cheap Fent Warehouse in Low Street; Briggs and Banks 'respectfully solicit the attention of a discerning public' to their improved washing, wringing and mangling machines; W. Town's Boot and Shoe Depot in Church Street sells the latest American over-shoes. Most noticeable are the Victorian preoccupations with home cures – Dr Airey's Celebrated Indian Pills, Balmforth's Vegetable Ointment, Fox's Anti-Cholera Mixture, Hudson's Essence of Aniseed, Naylor's Never-Failing Cure for Thick Necks – and with death: undertaker James Aked has a hearse 'with rich ostrich plumes', and will bury 'the poorer classes' for five shillings; grave-clothes maker Rebecca Buckley thanks the public 'for the very liberal support with which she has been favoured': William Chatburn of Upper Green supplies 'bride cakes and funeral biscuits on the shortest notice'; T. Dineen frames mourning cards 'after the French style.

Indeed, the atmosphere was ripe for Spiritualism which, crossing the Atlantic with an American visitor, manifested itself – for the first time in Yorkshire – at Keighley in the autumn of 1853, when thirteen enthusiasts contacted the spirits of a former Swedenborgian preacher and the poet Robert Burns. This they accomplished by table-rapping: John Hardacre was medium, one John Smith queried the apparently empty air, and somebody else ran a finger repeatedly over an alphabet. Smith's questions being met by unseen raps upon the table, the letters correspondingly pointed out on the alphabet were noted down, and answers thereby formulated. The process was slow and clumsy, but they were, they thought, in communication with spirits.

In the course of what must have seemed a rather tedious series of sittings, the late Swedenborgian gave them a sermon; Burns obliged with some posthumous verses:

When we wor in the world o' clay
We little ken'd how breef 'two'd be,
As carelessly we passed away
The time that wodna wait a wee …

When those early Spiritualists bravely published a pamphlet on their experiences, they were ridiculed, of course. 'Those authors,' facetiously observed *The Keighley Visitor*, 'who at their death left unfinished MSS are likely to complete them by means of spirit rapping!' Robert Burns replied with more verses and some rather feeble albeit topical riddles:

Question: 'Why is the Emperor of Russia like the clock?'
Answer: 'Because he is in the eleventh hour.'

A Society for Investigating the Phenomena of Spirit-Intercourse was founded, its rules defensive: 'Do you promise,' new members were asked, 'peaceably to withdraw if at any time you feel dissatisfied with the proceedings of this society?' In April, 1855, appeared *The Yorkshire Spiritual Telegraph*, published by J. Rhodes of Keighley Market and the first periodical of its kind in England, which continued variously monthly, weekly and fortnightly till incorporated in 1860 with the London *Spiritual Magazine*.

The town's first regular weekly newspaper, the *Keighley News* (no connection with the earlier venture of that name) began on April 5th 1862. Its proprietor was William Byles of *The Bradford Observer*, who regarded Keighley as 'a growing, thriving community, and ready for a paper of its own'; and its earlier four-page issues included national and foreign items, together with fiction ('Two Secrets, and How Disclosed: A Woman's Story'). The opening number reported a fire at 'Mr Sugden's mill', and locals were reputedly amazed that a Friday evening event could be read about first thing on Saturday morning! In politics, the *Keighley News* was Liberal. The next decade saw other ill-starred endeavours, the *Keighley Spectator* in

1868, and *The Keighley Daily Telegraph* — 'published every afternoon at 5 o'clock' — of 1870-1871; but it was 1873 before a rival weekly emerged in the shape of the Conservative *Keighley Herald*, which would survive until 1911.

To these years, too, belong a number of architectural and social features. Novelist Mrs Gaskell, gathering a quick impression while researching her biography of Charlotte Brontë, saw a Keighley 'in process of transformation from a populous, old-fashioned village, into a still more populous and flourishing town', and was struck by the 'solid grandeur' of its rows of grey stone houses. In 1853 the New Britannia Lodge of Oddfellows had built their imposing Britannia Hall in Market Street, which served as meeting-place and theatre, subsequently as Salvation Army headquarters ... On Shrove Tuesday, 1855, John Brigg laid the foundation-stone of the new Congregational chapel in Devonshire Street, which 'chaste and beautiful edifice', opened the following year, would see out the century as Keighley's possibly smartest church ... In 1858 came the improved Union Workhouse in Oakworth Road, later and kindlier known as Hillworth Lodge ... And on March 27th 1857 the Lord Bishop of Ripon consecrated the cemetery at Utley.

Benjamin Herschel Babbage in his Haworth report had read the locality a stern lesson on the dangers of old crowded burial-grounds surfaced with 'flat stones, laid at different heights from the ground, some of them simply reposing upon the mound of earth, which covers the grave': the practice was, he opined, 'a very bad one, as it prevents that access of atmospheric air to the ground, which is necessary for promoting decomposition; and, besides, the stones take the place of those grasses and shrubs which, if planted there, would tend to absorb the gases evolved during decomposition, and render the process less likely to contaminate the atmosphere'. In some urgency, then, Utley Cemetery was laid out on '£6,000 of borrowed money' – amongst the last burials in Keighley Parish churchyard was (none too soon, we might imagine) James Smith, a grocer who died on holiday at a temperance hotel in Germany and was brought leisurely and expensively ('they had £1 to pay for the Corps stoping at a house about 2 hours til the tide came up') home. For awhile thereafter, a public still unintroduced to parks took pleasure in 'walking round the Cemetery'.

By the 1861 census, Keighley's population was 21,859. The town itself had taken on a shape recognisable till at least the mid-twentieth century. To its staple worsted spinners and manufacturers were being added substantial numbers of ironfounders and machine-makers. From the station at East Parade ran trains 'nine times a day to all parts'. The parish boasted 'five episcopal and fourteen dissenting places of worship.' Its shops sold every commodity; straw hats, even, still in fashion, kept seven local women in business. In 1860, under the chairmanship of John Farrar Pickles, a Keighley Co-operative Society was formed.

The idea of working-class co-operation had been sown by a Keighley District Flour and Provision Society in 1854, which aimed 'to employ profitably the frugal means of its members by purchasing corn and other grain as cheap and good as possible, and to manufacture flour and meal for sale to its members'; this had failed, but its seed was ripe for germination. To Keighley a few years later came a fleeting and mysterious David Urquhart, described by contemporaries as 'a sort of disappointed politician' who 'had been out as a sort of attaché to the British Embassy in Turkey'.

Urquhart initiated two things in Keighley, both a trifle uncanny: a Foreign Affairs Committee and a Turkish Bath Company. Members of the former involved themselves with the Treaty of Paris after the Crimean War, and listed among their objects the chartering of 'an English vessel to convey the Circassian Deputies back to their homes without danger from the Russian Cruisers' (local treasurer for this quixotic scheme was Jonas Wells, the Greengate ironfounder). The Baths were situated in the Market, were run by one Sylvester Birtwhistle, and provided a venue for discussions on affairs in general. Both attracted like spirits, as epitomised by John Farrar Pickles, who had pioneered not only the ill-fated Flour Society but also the Land Society of the 1840s. This combination of circumstances and personalities produced the Keighley Co-operative Society. It was one of Urquhart's axioms 'that working men must not depend for help on the classes above them in the State, but must rely upon themselves for an improvement in the conditions of life'; or, as one founder member told his skimping young wife: 'We're going to have a "Co-op" Shop of our own. We're doing business for such as ye.'

The first handful of members wrote off to Rochdale for model rules, and tramped over to Hebden Bridge for flour. They struck 26,000 tin checks inscribed 'Keighley Store', had a signboard painted, bought their shopkeeper a pair of scales 'to weigh goods with when they come in'. Their first shop was in Church Green, their Committee-room in an attic so cramped they could barely stand up in it; in 1862 they moved into New Bridge Street. The treasurer took the takings home every night and hid them in a linen-chest. Once, when they overstocked with ham, they held a public tea in the Independent chapel to clear the surplus. Weathering a series of crises, the Keighley Co-operative Society branched out into drapery, bread-baking, china and pots, boots and clogs – and even opened a reading-room.

An interest in military matters also dates from 1860, when Keighley raised the 35th West Yorkshire Rifle Volunteer Corps, better known in its early days as the Aireworth Rifle Corps. Battalion headquarters were at Skipton. There was quite a craze for such organisations at the time (Poet Laureate Tennyson wrote a less than immortal poem with the refrain 'Riflemen, Riflemen, Riflemen form!'), though a humorous recruiting-poster signed by a pseudonymous 'Lorenzo Augustus Todlybags' suggests that local men needed prodding: 'Are your courage and patriotism to be twitted unchallenged by the "Sludgebumpers of Skipton" and their brethren in arms, "The Lime Galloway Cavalry of Lothersdale"!!' Form, however, they eventually did, paying for the privilege annual subscriptions ranging from five guineas to twelve shillings according to rank, and subject to fines for 'careless use of the Sword or Sword Bayonet, or for wounding with it any other Member of the Corps' and for 'discharging the Rifle accidentally'. By early 1861 they were ready for their first public appearance, marching 'in full uniform from the County Court to the Parish Church'; and a few months later created 'much excitement' by firing three volleys – into the air, it must hastily be added – at the funeral of one of their riflemen. By 1879 the Corps mustered a total strength of 162.

More specialist in its appeal was the Skating Club established in 1865, by whose efforts Redcar Tarn was transformed from a boggy mud-bath for cattle to a seven-acre sheet of water. Prominent founder-members were the Guard House Briggs who – future Mayors, magistrates, County Councillors and Members of Parliament – did their stint waist-deep in water sickling rushes. In the middle they left an island complete with a flag-pole: and at night, each skater would take his own lamp or candle, so that the Tarn must have resembled a gathering of fire-flies.

For more practical purposes, however, water was a sore subject in Keighley. The Company of Proprietors of the Waterworks had contrived to pipe a supply of sorts into the town, but the modest dimensions of their cisterns and their little reservoir at Calversyke Hill were ill-adapted to mid-century needs. The sizeable Keighley Moor Reservoir – colloquially the Big Dam – had been built in 1832 but supplied mill-owners only. The situation grew urgent in the 1860s, when Bradford turned envious eyes towards the potential resources of the Worth Valley. In 1867 the Keighley Local Board of Health commenced its possibly farthest-sighted undertaking by buying out the Company of Proprietors.

Its members had assumed a fearful responsibility, as emphasised by the following summer's drought. Piped water failed: Brunswick Street householders sent a deputation to a Board meeting to complain of being without for thirteen weeks. Machinery stood idle, factory supplies diverted for domestic use. The private Market pump was thrown open to the public. A well was sunk in Highfield Lane, but the fire-engine, set hopefully to work pumping it out, had drained it within twenty minutes. Springs up to a mile out of town were 'besieged night and day' by men, women and children with buckets and cans. 'Nothing – neither expense, covert opposition, nor open hostilities – will be deemed by the inhabitants an excuse for delay or even dilatoriness on the part of the Board,' a *Keighley News* correspondent voiced the universal view, 'they must let us have water, and they must let us have it soon'. Even the drains clogged and gave off 'poisonous gases' blamed in part for a scarlet fever epidemic, that autumn in 1868, which killed numbers of children.

The upshot was the Keighley Waterworks Extension and Improvement Act of 1869, and the construction of Ponden, Watersheddles and Blackhill Reservoirs. The statistics of such projects become hugely meaningless: Ponden Compensation Reservoir was 30 acres in extent, 49 feet deep, with a total capacity of 212,500,000 gallons ... Watersheddles Storage Reservoir (just over the Lancashire boundary, at the head of the Worth), 29 acres in extent, 52 feet deep, total capacity 190,663,200 gallons ... Blackhill Service Reservoir, dwarfed by comparison, 18 feet deep, total capacity a mere 2,500,000 gallons. The overall scheme was begun in 1870 and completed in 1878; its two main features, Ponden and Watersheddles, both took six years. Plans were even laid for the Lower Laithe works brought to fruition half a century later. Keighley's water supply was secured for generations.

Ponden Reservoir under construction in the early 1870s. This is the puddle-trench dug preparatory to building the embankment.

This alteration of the Victorian landscape was accomplished principally through the muscles and sweat of men and horses – especially men. The necessary army of navvies – for the Bradford Waterworks were concurrently building their Leeming and Leeshaw Reservoirs – poured into the district to write a rip-roaring chapter in the annals of sleepy hamlets like Scar Top and Stanbury and Leeming. They came together from all corners of the British Isles, and were nicknamed after their birthplaces: Cumberland, Devon and Derby, Chester, York and Lincoln, Leicester, Yarmouth, Dover and Cockney. They were traditionally fond of beef, bacon, and strong liquor. Some brought their wives, and some their women. For eight years they dug, drank, fought, whored, pilfered, were lamed and killed in puddle-trench mishaps. A shanty town sprang up at Scar Top. A row of twenty houses and cellar dwellings full of navvies at Leeming boasted 'one dirty, seatless, almost unapproachable little privy'. Stanbury people petitioned for an extra constable 'to keep the navvies in order'; in a royal free-for-all at Oxenhope they bested a self-styled 'King of Fighters of Denholme'. On the completion of Watersheddles Reservoir early in 1877, two hundred of them sat down to a celebration dinner while their employers toasted 'Success to the Keighley Waterworks, and Prosperity to the Town of Keighley'.

Chapter Six

Railways occasioned another of the Local Board of Health's concerns. In 1867 the Keighley and Worth Valley Railway Company, its mill-owning Directors alive to the need for good communications, opened its line from Oxenhope to join the Midland Railway at Keighley. This event has enjoyed a possibly disproportionate amount of notoriety by virtue of its commemoration by William Wright or Bill o' th' Hoylus End, man-about-town, poet, pamphleteer and, during the 1870s, compiler of a *Howorth, Cowenheead, and Bogthorn Almenak*; within days of the first train, he rushed out a little dialect prose-and-verse *History o' Haworth Railway*:

So strike up yor music an' give it sum maath,
An' welcum all nashuns fra north to th'saath;
Th'black fra th'east, an' th'red fra th'west,
For thay sud be welcum as weel as th'rest,
An' all beyond th'Tiber, th'Baltic, or Rhine,
Shall knaw at we've oppen'd th'Worth Valley Line.

By 1870, Keighley station was passing seven trains a day to Oxenhope, eleven to Skipton, and fourteen to Bradford and Leeds.

At that time, the station was situated to the north of East Parade and behind Cavendish Street, both the Midland and Worth Valley lines cutting Bradford Road by means of a level-crossing – an arrangement rendered proportionately less satisfactory as road and rail traffic increased: 'Yesterday we witnessed a scene which is common enough. More than a dozen people, besides vehicles and a herd of cattle, were kept standing in the road for five or ten minutes, not only while the regular trains passed, but while a long coal train was shunted up and down the siding'. Men having to cross the line on their way to work were likely to 'have to wait for passage until a fine at the works becomes inevitable'. Now, the provision of an alternative, though it might appear a comparatively minor business, would occupy the Local Board for a decade. There were discussions as to the relative merits of footbridges, roads going under railways, railways going under roads ... at last it was decided that Bradford Road should be carried by bridge over the lines. Even then, Keighley's Station Bridge was only accomplished, in 1879, after protracted wrangles with the Midland Railway Company and a Board deputation to a Parliamentary hearing, when member James Leach – that same Leach who had formerly served as a diary-keeping watchman, now turned greengrocer and broad-spoken, comical local politician – is credited with declaring: 'Ther's lots o' hosses been lamed at t' level crossin'. Why, Ah wor varry near jiggered mysel' one neet!'

Another problem arose in 1873, when the Great Northern Railway Company, preparing for a line from Halifax to Keighley, bought land at Low Bridge and thereby precluded further expansion of the gasworks. A handsome new gasworks was accordingly built at Thwaites, and opened on December 5th, 1876, by Benjamin Septimus Brigg, then Chairman of the Board. This highlights the two distinct classes of men now prominent in local affairs: on the one hand Mr Brigg,

The gasworks at Thwaites, opened in 1876.

manufacturer of Burlington House, who treated the Board and its officers to a six-course dinner at the Devonshire Hotel in honour of the occasion (the menu included such delicacies as calf's head, roast hare, and grouse); on the other, James Leach, familiarly called 'Pie', greengrocer of Low Street, pouring scorn on the gasworks commemorative plaque: 'He read for the edification of the members of the Board an inscription which he found cut in stone, announcing that they were opened in December, 1876, by Mr B.S. Brigg, and other particulars. He thought at first when he went in and saw that tombstone that he had got into the churchyard by mistake'. Even so, Mr Brigg contrived the last laugh: 'The Chairman remarked that he certainly had been ill, but had not yet, he was thankful to say, had his tombstone made'.

The old Low Bridge retort-house was subsequently adapted for use as the Fire Station; the pleasant little Gothic Revival railway station of 1847 continued in service till 1883, by which time the trains were too long for its platforms and it was superseded and re-sited; whilst the Great Northern Railway came to Keighley in 1884.

Chapter Six

Comparable, in its prolongation, with the building of Station Bridge, the Baths and Wash-houses affair began innocently enough in March, 1866, at the unpromising hour of ten o'clock on a Monday morning, when the Rector, the Revd William Busfeild, presided over a vestry meeting 'convened by the churchwardens, in compliance with a requisition signed by a number of rate-payers, to consider the propriety' of establishing public wash-houses for the town. The Rector reasonably observed that 'he believed that the object they had in view would tend to increase the health and comfort of the inhabitants generally'; and, were it not for the inherent seriousness of a ten-year delay, the unfolding project could be viewed as farce. The first years of the Baths and Wash-houses scandal are ineradicably coloured by what was termed a 'scurrilous caricature of the style and phraseology of the Holy Scriptures', which appeared in the *Keighley News* in December, 1869, under the title 'Chronicles of Wakefield (Compiled from Ancient MSS)', and was shortly reprinted as a pamphlet renamed, more explicitly, 'Chronicles of Keighley'. Its chapters and verses held local personalities up to merciless ridicule; its author remained anonymous, though contenders for that controversial honour include R.H. Hodgson, clerk to the Keighley magistrates who died as the result of an accident in 1876, and John Milligan, Fellow of the Royal College of Surgeons, Licentiate of the Society of Apothecaries, and Medical Officer of Health to the Keighley Local Board.

Born at Cross Hills in 1812, appointed first medical officer of the Keighley Union in 1838, a Mechanics' Institute member since 1842, Milligan was arguably the best brain in the town. As Vice-President of the Mechanics' Institute in 1847, he had revealed his especial concern by lecturing on 'Poverty as a Source of Disease, and Factory-Labour and Wool-Combing considered in relation to Health and Mortality'. Two years later, his essay 'On the Influence of Civilisation upon Health and Disease' won him the Fothergillian gold medal of the Medical Society of London. He contributed articles to *The Lancet*, experimented with 'a new mode of preserving vaccine lymph in glycerine', and, in partnership with John Smith, a Westgate watchmaker, invented – but never patented – an improved vaccination instrument. Litterateur and geologist, he assembled a varied library and a collection of Yorkshire fossils, rescued Keighley's old Market Cross from a scrap-yard and had it erected in his garden at Whinburn. As a poet, he turned out unconscionably dull works, though one of his livelier effusions is not without local interest insofar as it relates to the King Street Club-Houses murder of 1839:

With hands that shed a sister's gore,
His reeking blade cast on the floor,
The murderer quits his father's door:
Where'er he runs he runs with fear;
Where'er he looks are spectres there,
That eye him o'er with deadly glare,
And vicious glee!

His ambitious and well-nigh unreadable *Baal: or, Sketches of Social Evils*, published anonymously in 1861, had demonstrated his ability both to write in archaic style and to lampoon his enemies. If Milligan were indeed author of the *Chronicles*, he also carried on a lengthy, vituperative correspondence with himself in the *Keighley News* of early 1870, sending letters under both pseudonym and his own name; but, in an age of vigorous pamphleteering, this is by no means infeasible: as a professional man whose experience led him to regard baths and wash-houses as 'the most valuable sanitary institution' the town could acquire, he was effectively drawing attention to their delay. His obituary, in the *Keighley News* of March 11th 1876, guardedly mentions 'the sharp edge of his satirical knife' and, by an irony (or could it have been sly editorial design?), appears in the next column to an account of the 'preliminary opening of the Baths'.

But to return to the spring of 1866: a second vestry meeting – reputedly attended by only 'twelve or sixteen' enthusiasts – appointed seven Commissioners … or, as the *Chronicles* express it: 'Then the deacons of the temple called upon the people to assemble in an inner room of the sanctuary, and lo! there was only a small number met together, for the people understood not the matter. Nevertheless, the people then appointed certain of the elders of the city, who were to be called the Commissioners of the Baths and Washhouses'. After which, nothing happened till September the following year, when the Commissioners told another tiny vestry meeting that they had found a piece of land in Albert Street where, 'by the aid of a pump, they expected an efficient supply of water'; whereupon they were voted £6,000 out of the poor rates and 'began to build the baths and washhouses in the fourth month of the year, and on the first day of the month, which is called April'. In June, 1868, they requested, and were granted, a further £2,000, at a vestry meeting a mere dozen strong.

The storm broke in April, 1869, when 'the hewers of stone, and the workers of wood, and the drawers of water could not complete the works which they had in hand to do until more gold was provided for them', and the Commissioners asked for another £2,500. At last Keighley ratepayers were roused and, when the next vestry meeting was called, 'behold when the people were gathered together it was found that the inner room could not contain them, for the number was great. They, therefore, assembled in the ground which surrounds the sanctuary, and stood upon the graves of those who had been long dead'. This heated open-air meeting deferred voting any further money; whilst the newspaper report of the proceedings vies with the *Chronicles* in its appreciation of the ludicrous:

> 'The Chairman, who occupied a prominent position on the top of a gravestone, evidently became uncomfortable in his situation, and he called out: I wish you would move me out of the chair now.
>
> 'Mr Thomas Barnes: Move yourself out, you have done very badly in it.
>
> 'Mr Bottomley thereupon descended from his elevation, and the meeting soon afterwards dispersed.'

Chapter Six

Keighley Town Hall, built in 1901 and seen here decorated for the 1902 Coronation,

We need not follow the affair through all its ramifications; suffice it to say that for the next six years the half-built project stood idle whilst ratepayers split into 'bathites' and 'anti-bathites' tossed argument and abuse from one to another. Not till 1876 did the Baths and Wash-houses open – when 314 people tested the waters in the first four hours.

No sooner had the Baths and Wash-houses question left the stage, than the Board of Guardians took its place in the public eye. The Vaccination Acts of 1867 and 1871 had made its members responsible for enforcing the vaccination of the children within their Union – no easy burden, in the face of national opposition to what was still a controversial measure: In fact, the Guardians – in tune with the mood of the town – tacitly refused to prosecute the Acts. A Keighley smallpox epidemic in 1875 underlined the dangers of the situation, but also provided anti-vaccinationist propaganda insofar as both the vaccinated and the unvaccinated died. A long legal battle failed to budge the Guardians, until in August, 1876, the seven most obdurate among them were arrested, amid scenes of near-riot, as shouting crowds unhitched the horses from the omnibus taking them to the station, and dragged omnibus, Guardians and High Sheriff's officers round the streets. The occasion was celebrated locally with a brisk sale in carte-de-visite portraits of the prisoners, together with sundry broadsheets of verse:

At the pale little Sheriff one couldn't but smile,
As dumbfounded he sat like a mouse all the while;
Saying, I've heard tell o' Keighley, but ne'er been before,
And may I be hanged if I come any more.

The Guardians spent the better part of a month in the Debtors' Prison at York (the broadsheets more poetically said Clifford's Tower), where they ignored the rules, were fêted by the National Anti-Compulsory Vaccination League, showered with grapes, books and money from sympathisers, and finally released on bail at the fervent request of the harassed Governor. When, that November, the case of The Queen versus the Guardians of the Keighley Union came up at the High Court of Justice in London, the Vaccination Acts were at last applied: the obstinate seven returned home to tender their resignations and to receive a vote of thanks, endorsing a substantial public opinion, 'for the manner in which they have resisted the carrying out of compulsory vaccination in Keighley'.

Clearly, some of Keighley's steps up the ladder of civic progress were proving slow and painful. Its population – 21,859 in 1861, 28,059 in 1871, 33,540 in 1881 – included a rough element readily excited. Those traditional Yorkshire qualities of hard-headedness and sturdy individualism could accentuate a stubbornness rooted in ignorance, an exaggerated concern for the purse-strings, a natural antipathy to change.

As witness, again, the formation of the School Board...

Chapter Seven

School Board – Cottage Hospital – Oakworth House and Cliffe Castle – industry – Coffee House Company – societies and institutions – incorporation

The Elementary Education Act of 1870 authorised the setting up of locally-elected School Boards with powers to build schools, for children aged five to thirteen, where necessary – or, rather, advisable, since compulsion was not generally applied for another decade.

Existing tuition was provided by private, endowed and denominational schools. Keighley's private 'academies' mustered less than five hundred pupils between them. Its Free Grammar School boasted forty-two day scholars and six boarders, whose standard of reading, Latin and arithmetic was generally 'inferior', their spelling 'moderately' good. 'The boys,' commented a visiting Assistant Commissioner in 1865, 'are not supplied with suitable reading books'; much of their teaching was oral. Twenty small children in a dilapidated preparatory school were 'learning little or nothing'. Thirty-four pupils attended the Harehills Free School at Oakworth; its master, a former handloom-weaver, had been appointed because of his interest in Sunday School teaching, and did 'not consider himself competent, even if the school improves, to teach anything except reading, writing, and arithmetic'. The Church of England, the Roman Catholics and the Nonconformists had all established schools; they accommodated, respectively: St Anne's Roman Catholic School, 140; St Mary's National School, 295; Oakworth National School, 214; Oakworth Wesleyan School, 457; Keighley National School, 755; Ingrow National School, 341; Keighley Wesleyan School, 437; and Laycock Wesleyan School, 191 – overall accommodation, 2,830. In 1875, denominational school registers netted 3,749 names: the 'average attendance' was 2,007. An apparent discrepancy is explained by the fact that 2,144 pupils were factory half-timers, different sets attending morning and afternoon. The total number of children aged between five and thirteen in Keighley, in 1875, was 4,826.

The log-book of Oakworth Wesleyan School, in the 1860s, speaks graphically of the tribulations of a succession of masters – Francis J. Sutton, William Preston,

Charles Gardner, John Rowe – who, with a few pupil-teachers, struggled to instil even a modicum of learning. Their half-timers persistently came late ('Our clock is considerably before the factory clock; this is the cause of many coming late'), and they came dirty ('But owing to the distance some of them have to come there is very little time to attend to toilet matters and to get their dinners'), or they did not come at all ('Messrs Sugden's mill stopped – its half-timers mostly absent'). Classes fluctuated with the weather; some stayed away at hay-time; others refused to pay the school fee of a penny a week. One lad went 'to another school because he thought he had too much work here'; another unruly character 'told his parents today that he would not come, and is now playing at home, being his own and his parents' master'. Teachers sometimes 'spoke to children about trying to get new scholars'; and one eager new arrival reported: 'In the evening from 4 to 5 with pupil-teachers visited houses on Chip Hill to see if any new scholars could be got'.

Having assembled a reasonable number of pupils, the masters' trials had scarcely begun. 'Find it very difficult to teach children in the same class for all subjects,' Francis Sutton admitted early in 1863. Children 'experienced trouble through the desks being so light & not fixed to the floor'. Bright sunlight created problems 'for want of blinds'. Fires went out. One day everybody was 'very much tormented with mice running across the floor, notwithstanding the noise'. Even Her Majesty's Inspector, in his 1868 Report, remarked in his roundabout way 'that the offices for the two sexes should have separate approaches'. The masters themselves, not perhaps of the first water, were patently over-strained: 'Gave a boy a push yesterday in the gallery falling over the back of the seat his nose was made to bleed – I have resolved not to push any one again. The lad had misbehaved & spoke very rudely'. (This master was Charles Gardner, who did not last very long; but he was also the man who could write: 'The weather was so genial I took the elder scholars for an hour's run in the afternoon'.)

Yet whatever the shortcomings of Keighley's elementary education – and contemporary writers speak of failures 'both in the quality and quantity of the instruction generally given' – no School Board would form for another five years, a delay rendered the more glaring by contrast with educational developments in other fields.

By 1864 the Keighley Mechanics' Institute was mooting the question of a new and 'more commodious' building. Its Library then numbered 3,362 volumes, its news-room took thirty-one newspapers and periodicals, its membership totalled 445; whilst a drawing class (held in that same basement which had earlier housed the librarian) had been recognised as a branch of the Leeds School of Art. Several features, envisaged for an abortive Town Hall scheme about the same time, were incorporated into the proposed Mechanics' Institute, which emerged as a complex of classrooms, studios and committee-rooms, with library, exhibition gallery, and public hall to hold 1,200. Two years in the building, the 'handsome Gothic structure' was opened by the Duke of Devonshire on 30th September 1870. Conspicuously sited in the angle of Cavendish Street and Skipton Road, Keighley Mechanics' Institute would dominate the town for nearly the next century.

Chapter Seven

Above: *Turn-of-the-century North Street, with the Mechanics' Institute clock tower in the background.*

Right: *Keighley Mechanics' Institute poster, advertising a lecture by Titus Salt, 1871.*

MECHANICS' INSTITUTION
KEIGHLEY.

The Committee have great pleasure in announcing that on

Wednesday, November 8th, 1871,

A

LECTURE

Will be given in the above Hall, by

TITUS SALT, ESQ.,

(OF SALTAIRE),

SUBJECT:

"REMINISCENCES OF A TOUR IN EGYPT AND THE HOLY LAND,"

Illustrated by Coloured Photographs of all the principal places of interest, and by

PERSONS DRESSED IN ORIENTAL COSTUMES.

The Photographs will be exhibited by the

OXY-HYDROGEN LIME LIGHT.

THE CHAIR WILL BE TAKEN BY

I. HOLDEN, ESQ., J.P.

ADMISSION: Front Seats 1s., Second Seats 6d., Gallery 3d.

Members of the Institution, on showing their Cards, admitted at half fees, to Second and Third Seats

Doors open at Half-past Seven, Lecture to commence at Eight.

THOMAS CARRODUS, Secretary.

J. L. CRABTREE, PRINTER AND STATIONER, KEIGHLEY.

Immediately, the Institute became the centre of what almost amounted to a social and cultural frenzy. Balls, concerts, lectures, operettas, flower shows, conversaziones, oratorios, readings, Saturday-Night Entertainments vied one with another for a share of a boundless public patronage. A succession of notable names mounted the Keighley platform. Charles Hallé brought a small orchestra to a Full Dress Concert. Actor George Grossmith gave his rendition of *David Copperfield*. Gerald Massey lectured on 'Charlotte Bronte', Lord William Lennox on 'Personal Reminiscences of Wellington'. Ben Preston, now remembered as a dialect poet, was then billed as 'the Yorkshire Humourist' and brought the house down. Titus Salt, in 1871, obliged with his 'Reminiscences of a Tour in Egypt and the Holy Land', illustrated by means of 'persons dressed in Oriental Costumes' and coloured photographs 'exhibited by the Oxy-Hydrogen Lime Light'. Fresh in 1887 from the battlefields of Empire came Melton Prior, war artist of the *Illustrated London News*, with a lantern lecture on 'The Soudan War and Nile Expedition'. The Institute Dramatic Class performed their highly-flavoured *Eugene Aram*, complete with programme notes explaining the whole tear-jerking tale: 'The Condemned Cell – Aram's Confession – Affecting interview between Aram and Madeline — Death of Madeline — Aram's last soliloquy and Death — Affecting Tableau'.

But the new building enjoyed further-reaching advantages: the former basement drawing class transferred fully-fledged as a School of Science and Art 'in connection,' its brochure emphasised, 'with the Science and Art Department, South Kensington, and with the Society of Arts'. Meanwhile, the Endowed Schools Commissioners were revising their use of the John Drake and Jonas Tonson funds, pensioning off the old Grammar School masters and, instead, subsidising new boys' and girls' schools: the former opened in the Mechanics' Institute in 1871 as a Trade School offering 'a liberal and practical English education, supplemented by the systematic teaching of such Art and Science subjects as are applicable to the trades of the district'; the latter, the Drake and Tonson's School for girls, commenced in Strawberry Street early the following year. At a stroke, almost, had been laid the foundations of the Technical College and the Boys' and Girls' Grammar Schools.

What was more, an educational champion was evolving in the form of an ambitious but diffident young businessman called Swire Smith. 'I only lack ability,' he had wistfully confided to his diary in 1867, 'in order to be locally powerful'; and had had to be strongly persuaded to undertake the secretaryship of the Mechanics' Institute drawing class in which capacity, speaking at the 1870 prize-giving, he opined that 'Keighley is at present pretty well supplied with elementary schools'. But the next few years would see a development and a change in Swire Smith. In 1872 he made one of a party from the Committee of the Keighley Institute and Trade School (the others were John Brigg, John Clough, E.D.A. Marriner, and L.C. Miall of Leeds) who visited Germany and Switzerland 'with the object of studying recent improvements in the building and management of schools'. He came home, not only committed to a distinguished career in technical education, but also alive to the deficiencies of local elementary schooling. 'I have heard in Keighley,' he wrote in his *Educational Comparisons* published on his return, 'of

Sir Swire Smith (1842-1918), from a portrait by Solomon J. Solomon, R.A.

classes taught in the outer porch of the school because of the great crowd within, and I have seen a class assembled in the playground in order to escape the vitiated air and the Babel-like noise which I could hear going on inside. The head teacher of an elementary school in Keighley told me not long ago that many children come to school at ten or eleven who do not know their letters, and many leave at the age of thirteen unable to read or write'.

Thus it transpired that, on New Year's Day, 1873, in a town still – in the third year after the Elementary Education Act – innocent of a School Board, this man who had shyly thought himself a 'woful disappointment' as a lecturer, stood in the Mechanics' Institute and minced no words: 'children were attending school and not learning, and although the school door might be open, there were many neglected children who never went in, but received as their only teaching the pernicious education of the street and the gutter'. The *Keighley News* followed up with a leader headlined 'Elementary Education in Keighley', and commented: 'Mr Smith has given the people of Keighley a New Year's lesson by which we hope they will profit'.

Unhappily, the climate of the times, anti-Baths and Wash-houses, anti-vaccination, was also predictably anti-School Board. The opposition replied in typical fashion with cheap broadside wit:

Dandy Swire went o'er the sea,
Right away to Germany;
'Sure I'm travelled now,' quoth he —
And he was, was Dandy.

Back he came; chokeful was he
With a brand-new bright idee.
'Now I'll make a noise,' said he:
So he did, the Dandy …

Give it up; we don't agree;
Get a wife to play with thee —
Or else go live in Germanie,
Pretty Swire, the Dandy!

(The latter stanza was a gibe at Smith's life-long bachelorhood and his rather notable lack of success with the opposite sex.) There followed a long and extremely verbose School Board correspondence in the *Keighley News*, mounting in aggressiveness week by week, until the editor was fain to call a halt; out of which excitable welter of pros and cons, one letter shines with a simple dignity. It was signed 'A Mechanic':

> Sir, – I am a working man and belong to a poor denomination that cannot afford to build a school. Hundreds of others are in the same position and we think there should be a school in the town that belongs to the ratepayers so that we shall not keep hearing that this church or chapel is paying for our children's schooling. I have long thought the present schools are not as they should be, and I judge by results. Where I work there is scores of young men who went to the National, or Methodist or Catholic school till they were 13, and a many of them can hardly write their names and to hear them talk all day long is awful. Many of them hardly ever speak without swearing, and they sing songs that is not fit to hear. They have no decency and women and girls having to live in the same houses get into bad habits also. They would not be like this if they were better educated. The hundreds of children who don't go to school are growing up corrupted … Improvement is wanted and we cannot begin too soon. It is us working men who suffer by delay and the battle that Mr Swire Smith and the Messrs. Summerscale Bros. are fighting is our battle not theirs … I am a convert to a School Board.

That summer, the issue, acquiring political undertones with Liberals for, Conservatives against, was roisterously put to the vote. At an open-air meeting at Exley Head, 'a huge dead rat found its way on to the shoulders of one of the opposition speakers', whilst a 'missile of some size' narrowly missed Smith's head and scored 'a severe blow upon the left shoulder' of the *Keighley News* reporter. The School Board was defeated by 540 votes to 2026: at one polling-booth, 122 out of 194 voters could not write their names.

Chapter Seven

But the 1870 Act had included a clause for compelling the formation of a School Board in districts failing to meet minimum requirements, and eventually Parliament and the Education Department heard about Keighley's plight, through a District Inspector's report – 'in one school not one of the first class knew the name of the county they lived in; in another the only boy who ventured to say where London was put it in Wales' – and ordered a School Board. So the town voted again on March 31st 1875, under a deluge of posters, pamphlets, broadsheets, lampoons ... the opposition now entering the contest to preserve as far as possible the 'status quo' ('We will not allow the rate-payers' money to be squandered in pinnacle ornamentations as in Leeds, Bradford and elsewhere'), the supporters perforce electioneering along similar lines ('We are anxious to provide a good education for all the children of the district, at the cheapest possible cost to the Rate-payers'), and the versifiers exhorting both sides to the polls:

Stand by Frederick and Laycock, and gallant young Swire!
Let these noble champions the loyalty fire
Of patriot son and patriot sire
And yours is the day!

This time, faced with the inevitability of a School Board, the fickle public voted a resounding victory for the men whom they had defeated two years before: Swire Smith came out top of the poll; the rest included a ubiquitous Clough, Sugden, Laycock and Summerscales. Once in office, rate-payers' money or no, they went to work with a will. Within the first four years of their existence they opened six Board Schools, at Eastwood, Oakworth, Utley, Oldfield, Holycroft and Worth Village.

Not the least striking aspect of the mid-Victorian era is this extreme briskness with which its more prominent citizens could act when opportunity or need arose. Early in 1873, hearing of War Office plans to establish an Army camp on Rombalds Moor, Keighley's 'employers of labour, ministers of religion, and other inhabitants' joined their Ilkley counterparts in a spirited programme of public meetings, petitions and deputations to the Secretary of State for War, which squashed the project within weeks – this despite the opposition of local publicans, tradesmen, Volunteers and young women of the more adventurous sort, who favoured the camp. The episode threw up some illuminating quotations: 'No military centre can be established anywhere without bringing in its train evils on which no pure imagination willingly rests' (a *Keighley News* leading article); 'The small drapers in Leeds and Bradford of twenty years ago have grown large drapers, and strut about on Sundays, and they do not like to think of the soldiers coming to take their places' (Captain Brown of Keighley lambasting the residents of Ilkley); 'It's ruination to any town where they come' (an old soldier on his former comrades-in-arms).

The town could also bestir itself (though not quite so energetically) in more positive directions, as in the founding of its hospital. Prior to 1876, local casualties had to be taken to Bradford Infirmary, 'they being,' according to contemporary account, 'very much injured by this system' – one is grimly reminded of a Bingley boiler explosion in 1869, when an engine-tenter with a fractured thigh, broken ribs and torn lungs was jolted off to Bradford 'on an open cart': he died, of course. At a meeting discussing the problem in 1874, Keighley's future Medical Officer of Health, Arthur Roberts, said of Bradford Infirmary 'that the patients who had met with accidents in Keighley often went down so debilitated from loss of blood that it was almost impossible for them to recover, and that frequently they died from blood poisoning.' A hospital committee was accordingly formed which, in the summer of 1876, opened the Keighley Cottage Hospital, 'essentially intended for the treatment of Surgical emergencies of those persons engaged in the industrial occupations or calling of life (including domestic servants), who, when overtaken by accident, are unable to obtain that accommodation, care, and attention, which the more affluent can command, and the destitute have by law provided for them'.

The Cottage Hospital originally rented a house built by the late Aaron Iveson, a prosperous draper, in Highfield Lane, then a 'convenient distance from the town' and occupying a suitably 'salubrious position'. The kitchen table was used for operations. It had a matron, with a girl to help her; a management committee of three ladies; and local doctors attended free of charge. There were eight beds but, in the first few years, usually only two to five patients at a time – who could be expelled if 'using profane or abusive language, or guilty of improper conduct, or using spirituous liquors', and were supposed to 'assist the nurse and their fellow patients when required'. Of twenty-nine admitted during 1878, twenty-six were 'successfully treated', two 'discharged considerably improved', and one died. Funds were raised 'by the payments of the patients and their friends' (though those early patients seem to have paid nothing), and by voluntary contributions.

The first few years were a financial struggle, despite subscriptions from firms and individuals. Most churches and chapels held special collections, but by April of 1877 the grand total of these, since 1874, had reached a not particularly spectacular £114 16s 2d. A Charity Ball at the Mechanics' Institute raised only £61 6s, although tickets cost a guinea for gentlemen and 10s 6d for ladies. Smaller amounts arrived from less orthodox sources: 'Mr Jonathan Whitley, Scott Street, honorary secretary to the Keighley Cottage Hospital, begs to acknowledge the receipt of 9s from Mr Adam Pollard, manufacturer, Greengate, being amount of fines from work people for disobedience to rules'; whilst the 'committee for illuminating the dials of Keighley Parish Church clock', having achieved their object with £1 1s 2d to spare, passed on the surplus. More usefully, local friendly societies hit upon the happy notion of simultaneously raising Cottage Hospital funds and parading their strength: their first procession and entertainments, in 1877, succeeded in spite of wet weather. 'It is to be hoped,' commented the *Keighley Herald* with some prescience, 'that this will not be the only one; but that the result of Saturday's gala will encourage the promoters to make it one of the annual institutions of the town'. And such has proved the case.

Chapter Seven

That first Friendly Societies' procession mustered (by permission) in the grounds of Cliffe Castle and disbanded at Eastwood House, for the smoky town was richly environed with substantial residences and parklands. To be sure, the manors and yeoman dwellings of earlier centuries – East and West Riddlesden Halls, Laycock Manor, Haworth Old Hall – were still seeing largely workaday service as farms; but the comparatively modest homes of earlier industrialists, like The Knowle, Cliffe Hall, Aireworth House, were in process of being outshone by later Victorian magnates. None would ever better the classical dignity of William Sugden's Eastwood House, built in 1819 on the 'field of plain earth' where Miles Gale had watched horse-racing; but not for want of effort or expense. Joseph Henry Craven's Strong Close ranked as the second most costly house in Keighley. Its position was low and its views limited, however, so Mr Craven encircled his adjacent Dalton Mills chimney 'with a kind of tower, rising nearly as high as the chimney, and from the various points of this tower distant views may be obtained'. Three miles away, Isaac Holden, a Scots-born cotton piecer who had worked his way up to become master of an extensive combing concern and Member of Parliament for the North-West Riding Division, was developing Oakworth House into the Worth Valley's 'principal attraction'. Its massive architecture was described as 'in the Italian style'. French artists painted its interior decorations; French workmen built its rockeries; Italian craftsmen laid the mosaic floors of its half-acre winter garden costing £30,000. Even the adjoining Wesleyan Chapel, 'which was liberally subscribed for by Mr Holden', acted as 'an ornamental and useful appendage'. On Saturdays and holidays the grounds were opened to the public – until the depressingly inevitable 'damage done to the property' curtailed this privilege.

Yet it was Cliffe Castle which emerged 'undoubtedly', by contemporary, estimate, 'one of the finest residences which have been constructed in Yorkshire, or even the whole Kingdom, during the last decade'. This was due to Henry Isaac Butterfield, whose firm Butterfield Brothers enjoyed a flourishing worsted trade with the United States, and whose wife, niece of Judge Roosevelt of New York, had merited inclusion in a book called *Queens of American Society*: she had been presented at court, and had preferred living in Paris, where her 'personal beauty, her natural grace, her many accomplishments (being a fine linguist), and her exquisite taste .... added to her husband's wealth and liberality, soon gave her a prominent position in the court circles of that brilliant capital'. She had died, not yet thirty, in 1867.

In 1875 Henry Isaac Butterfield began his eight-years' rebuilding of Cliffe Hall, the mock-Elizabethan family home along the Skipton road. Its elevation of title to Castle was no empty figure of speech: the huge towered and turreted structure was variously described as 'a modernised Tudor castle in the Victorian era', and 'a good specimen of the Elizabethan castellated style of architecture'. It cost an estimated £130,000, and its estate stretched 'nearly to the village of Steeton', whilst its more immediate grounds included marble fountains 'in the Florentine style' and conservatories growing bananas and grapes. A man of cosmopolitan tastes, who

Henry Isaac Butterfield's Cliffe Castle.

spent much of his time abroad, Butterfield filled his Castle with treasures. There was a fireplace of malachite mined in Siberia, a Louis XIV card-table, a 'unique' time-piece from the Paris Exhibition, and a tea-caddy that had belonged to the late Emperor Napoleon III. Two Chinese vases had been literally looted from the Summer Palace at Peking in 1860 – Count Palikao, French commander in the China War, was father-in-law of Butterfield's niece. Tucked away amongst walls of pictures (one group of deer, 'after Landseer', being of notably 'large dimensions') was a Paul Veronese. Mr Butterfield's bedroom furniture had formerly been Rossini's, and he had the dubious satisfaction of sleeping in the bed 'on which that eminent composer had passed away to his rest'.

If the wider populace had to accept vastly more frugal conditions, if Keighley still harboured its squalid rookeries and its accumulating chimneys poured forth an ever-thickening pall, the town was nonetheless struggling clear of the raw brutalities of the previous generation. By 1881, population 33,540, a recognisable plan had taken shape. The sober lines of Devonshire Street and others named substantially after Liberal politicians — Argyll, Granville, Spencer, Campbell, Russell — were pushing uphill across former nursery gardens to the west of North Street. Highfield Lane, distinguished, thirty years before, only by a. brewery, was becoming residential. Northwards along Skipton Road grew, on the left hand, villas, on the right hand, streets. Solid rows of homes with pretty bird names like Plover, Thrush, Linnet and Dove Street, marched along the Eastwood House

A smoky townscape of Keighley chimneys in the 1870s.

boundary-wall. Buildings spreading steadily outwards were connecting the town proper with Ingrow and Fell Lane, Guard House and Worth Village.

Industry was booming. Machine-makers and ironfounders (George Hattersley & Sons, Prince Smith & Son) and machine-tool makers (Darling & Sellers; Hall & Stell; Dean, Smith & Grace) expanded conveniently amongst worsted spinners and manufacturers (J. & J. Craven & Co., B. & W. Marriner, John Brigg & Co., William Lund & Son) whose seventy mills in 1879 aggregated 6,452 looms and 301,580 spinning and doubling spindles: this, it was alleged, amounted to 'one tenth of the mills, nearly one-eighth of the spindles, and nearly one-twelfth of the looms employed in the worsted trade throughout the United Kingdom'. Keighley had also emerged pre-eminent in the manufacture of washing-machines, wringers and mangles (William Summerscales and Sons; Whalley, Smith and Paget; Holmes, Pearson and Midgley), together with associated agricultural implements such as chaff cutters, oil cake breakers, turnip pulpers and currant cleaners, and with sewing-machines – William Sellers and Sons' 'Stitchwell' boasted 'a world-wide reputation'. Specialist trades abounded: Clapham Brothers casting gas and water pipes, Verity and Shuttleworth preparing ready-made joinery, Hoyle and Wright bottling aerated waters. J. B. Beadman & Co. built railway wagons; Sagar and Broughton made cart covers and horse sheets; Spencer Brothers advertised a cattle spice 'strongly recommended for purifying the blood of all Animals, stimulating the Digestive Organs, greatly increasing the Appetite, and enabling the Animals to

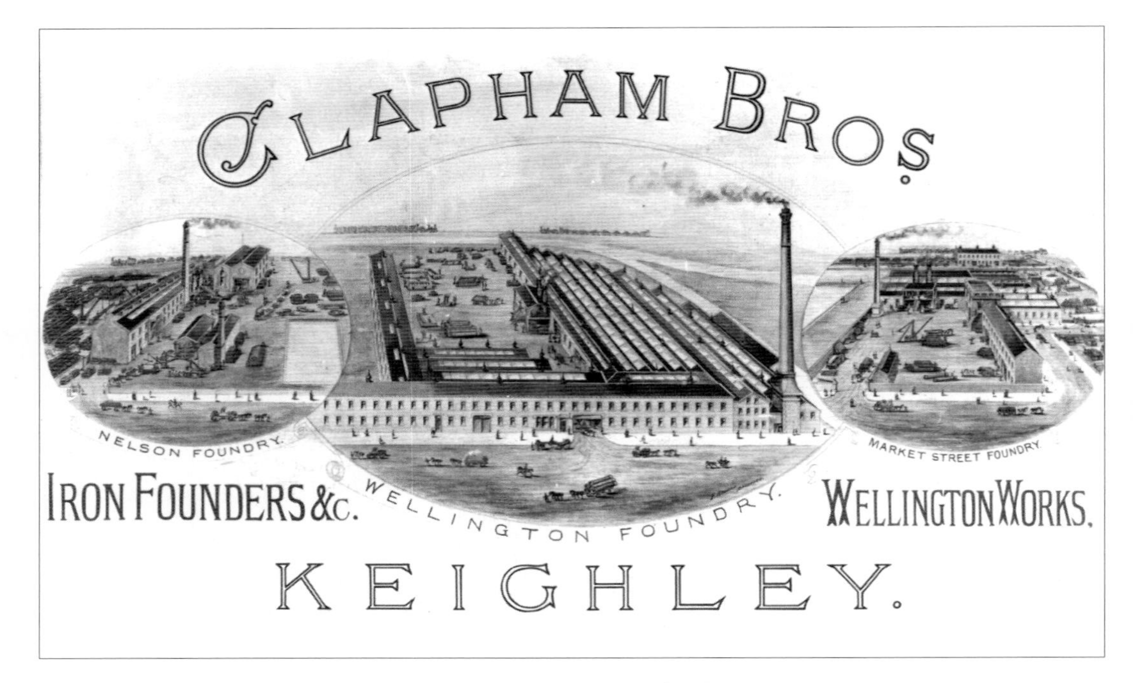

Late Victorian industry: letterhead illustrating Clapham Bros foundries.

assimilate a much greater quantity of food, while keeping them in perfect health'. Directories reveal a versatile amalgam of manufactures: mattresses, Venetian blinds, soap, washing liquid, files, baskets, boot protectors, sauce, rope, tobacco pipes, brushes.

The community was bustlingly alive, variously textured with social activities. The craze of the day was the coffee house. Keighley's first, the Acorn in Low Street, had refreshment rooms wallpapered with medieval patterns, where customers sat at marble-topped tables drinking coffee, cocoa and tea 'at extremely low prices'; newspapers and magazines were provided. This was the project of a Coffee House Company formed by the town's clergy and philanthropists; for, as John Brigg expressed it at the opening ceremony in 1878: 'Men had distinct social instincts, which induced them to collect in numbers; and he held that drunkenness, one of our most glaring vices, had been fostered more by man's social leanings and habits than by almost any other single cause. In this and kindred places of refreshment, however, they had the means of indulging these instincts without risk of impairing their faculties or making beasts of themselves'. After which, Mr Brigg drank the first cup of coffee, 'and the waitresses were found their work for the next half-hour'. For the more energetic, the Mechanics' Institute yard housed a roller skating rink and a gymnasium stocked with parallel and horizontal bars, jumping and vaulting horses, dumb-bells and Indian clubs.

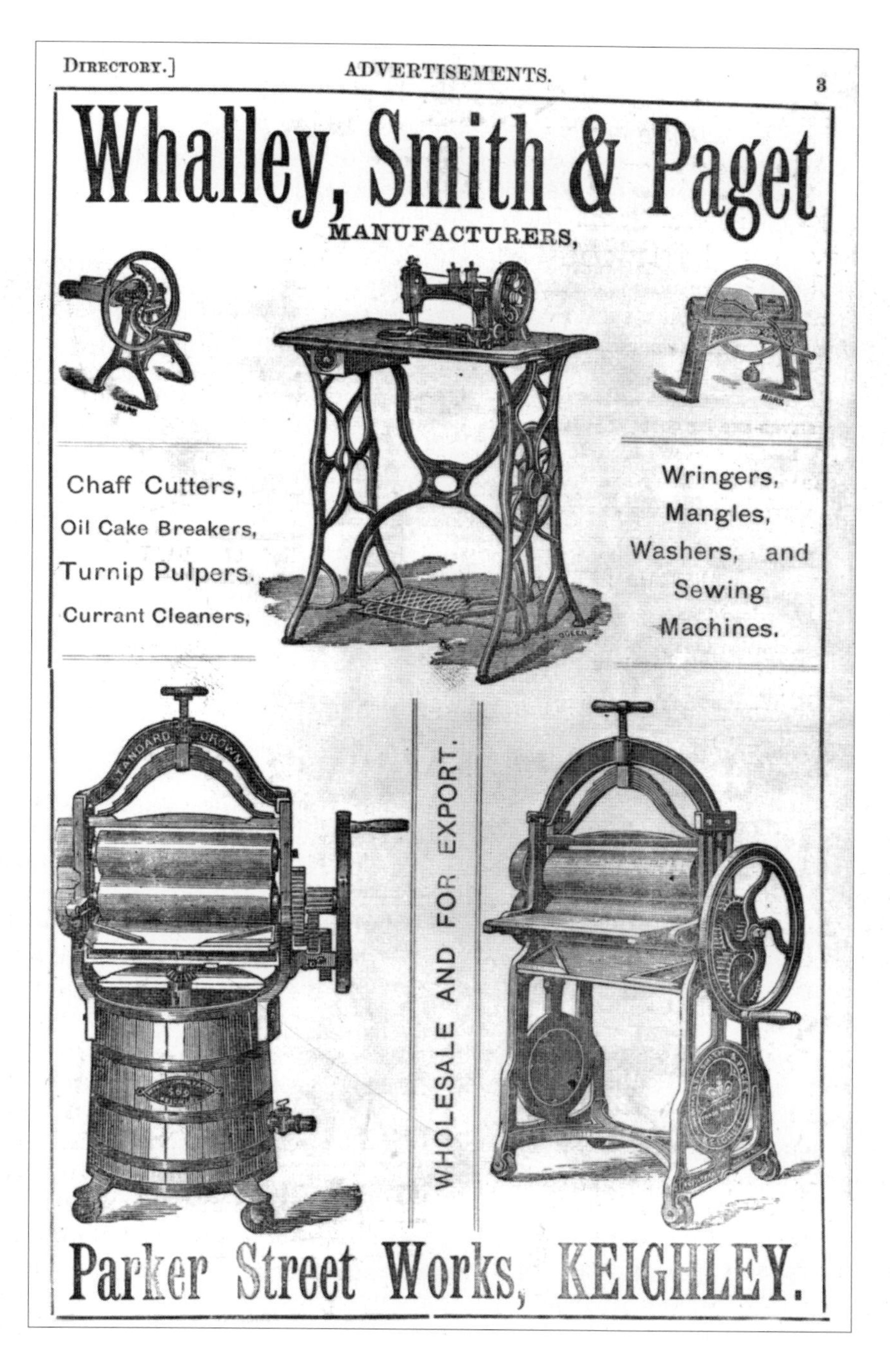

A range of wholesale and export manufactures advertised by Whalley, Smith & Paget of Parker Street Works in 1884.

At Easter in 1880 Abraham Kershaw, a piano-tuner from Huddersfield who had been experimenting with a home-made Theatre of Varieties, opened his wooden five-storey Queen's Theatre and Opera House in Queen Street (which the *Keighley News*, in the high-flown journalism of the era, described as 'a temple devoted exclusively to the worship of Thespis and the Muses'). Its standard backdrop represented Lake Geneva; against which, to a disappointing first-night audience, the Leeds Harmonic Union Quartette Party gave a concert and was by the interval reduced to a trio, one Walter Singleton's voice having failed during a song from *Carmen*. The following week, the Travcrner's Opera Company's first performances of *Il Trovatore* attracted sparse attendances; but at least Keighley now boasted what the *Herald* called 'an innocent place of amusement'.

Societies were springing up. A Football Club founded in 1876 – 'the rules are those of the Association and Rugby Union' – was lent a field at Lawkholme Lane. The Eastwood House lawn became the setting for a more select Tennis Club. An Angling Club fished the Aire between Stockbridge and Eastburn. A Botanic Society established in 1868 broadened its interests to include birds, animals and insects, and became the Naturalists' Society. Gardeners of a specialist bent could join the Gooseberry Growers' Association, and the Worth Valley Hotel at Ingrow held an annual Gooseberry Show; the Globe Inn, not to be outdone, boasted a Celery Show. Musical talents found a variety of outlets: a Musical Union, developed from the Choral Society of forty years earlier, was thought to possess 'one of the best and most valuable libraries of music in Yorkshire', whilst a recent Amateur Choral Society and a Church Institute Choral Society vied with one another through a succession of glees and part-songs. W. Lister Marriner's Private Brass Band, uniformed and equipped at its founder's expense, had been winning prizes since 1855, as far afield as the Crystal Palace; the St Peter's School Brass Band trained potential recruits. Other firm or family concerns included Haggas's, Spencer's Quadrille, and Redman's Orchestral Bands. A Military Reed Band played 'both brass and wood instruments'; and a Concertina Band formed in 1873 proved so popular that the Model and the Star Concertina Bands soon followed suit. The Parish Church and the Park Lane Hand-Bell Ringers pealed their way round relevant contests of the neighbourhood.

There was a Working Men's Club in Park Lane, and a Cavendish Club for 'the most influential gentlemen of the town' adjoined the Devonshire Arms. The Sandywood Club had taken over an old cotton mill in Skipton Road; its shareholders, baulked in a scheme to open a hotel, had settled for billiards and bowls, the rear of their premises laid out with a green surrounded by trees and shrubs, 'which give it a very pretty appearance'. A Conservative Club was established in 1875, a Liberal Club in 1876, both lagging slightly behind a Home Rule Club of 1874 pledged 'to assist to obtain for Ireland, by all legitimate means, the right of managing her own internal affairs'. A Radical Club sought, amongst its predictable objects, 'Parliamentary franchise for Keighley'.

Only some 1,400 householders were eligible to vote at Parliamentary elections, and Keighley simply constituted part of the Northern Division of the West Riding,

Chapter Seven

The Queen's Theatre and Opera House after being rebuilt in brick and stone in 1889.

returning no Member of its own – the whole of Yorkshire was represented by only thirty-eight Members of Parliament. Twice, in 1867 and 1879, abortive attempts had been made to establish Keighley as a Parliamentary borough; on the former occasion, the Parish Church bells had been rung in premature expectation of a victory. The matter was raised again at a Local Board meeting in September of 1881, when that old watchman and rough wit, James Leach, proposed the calling of a public meeting 'to take into consideration the incorporation of Keighley, and thereby to ascertain whether it would be better to be incorporated or to remain under a Local Board of Health'; which, largely attended in the Mechanics' Institute the following month, heartily endorsed a resolution moved by Benjamin Septimus Brigg:

> That, in the opinion of this meeting. the time has now come when the town of Keighley (which for the last twenty-six years has been a district constituted under the Public Health Acts, and for thirty-one years previously thereto a district under Improvement Commissioners) should endeavour to attain the highest form of local government.

Leach seconded and quoted some vaguely appropriate lines from Bill o' th' Hoylus End:

Nivver dee i' thi shell, owd lad.
Bud let thi motto be, –
'Onward!' an' 'Excelsior';
An' try for t'top o' t'tree.

Just two dissenting hands were raised.

This time, no reference was made to Parliamentary representation, and the solely municipal Charter of Incorporation passed steadily through due legal forms to gain the assent of the Lords of the Privy Council on July 28th 1882. At the time, Keighley received its change of status with the utmost coolness, the only documented reaction being an enquiry as to how much the incorporation would cost; George Burr, Clerk to the Local Board and shortly to become Keighley s first Town Clerk, 'replied that he was unable to state definitely, but he thought £250 would cover all the expenses.'

Chapter Eight

Borough coat of arms – telephone exchange – electricity – Tramways Company – public parks – museum – public library – Members of Parliament – South African War – Freemen of the Borough – local personalities – engineers' strike

The newly-fledged borough occupied the same area as its predecessor the Local Board, a one-mile radius from the Devonshire Hotel, plus a scrap of land for the gasworks at Thwaites and minus a strip down the Hog Holes Beck, from Glen Lee to the Worth, belonging to Bingley – who also owned Hainworth and part of Ingrow. Oakworth retained its own Local Board, whose jurisdiction extended round the west of the town to include Utley; even Keighley's Cemetery lay outside its boundary.

That autumn of 1882, the first Town Council was elected, in a day of steady polling when 'there was at no time any heavy pressure at any of the booths'. By way of commemoration, workers were told that 'they were quite at liberty to stay away' from work during the afternoon. The extrovert Leach had got himself nominated in five of the six wards, but the voting public registered their estimate of his worth by placing him bottom of the poll in two wards and next to the bottom in the other three. The eighteen successful Councillors, out of thirty-nine candidates, comprised five manufacturers (B.S. Brigg, Ira Ickringill, John Haggas, William Clough and E.D.A. Marriner), two machine-makers (John Spencer and R.L. Hattersley), two gentlemen, two contractors, an auctioneer, an ironmonger, a spirit merchant, a decorator, a greengrocer, a woolcomber and a coal dealer. Nine of them had served on the last Local Board of Health. Benjamin Septimus Brigg became Keighley's first Mayor; Richard Longden Hattersley, who had also been strongly tipped for the honour, succeeded him the following year.

The Borough coat of arms was granted by the Heralds' College early in 1883: 'Argent on a Fesse Sable, between three Stags' heads caboshed a Fountain proper, all within a Bordure embattled Azure. And for the Crest on a Wreath of the Colours, in front of a Dragon's head erased Gules, entwined by a Serpent Or, a

Fountain proper'. In layman's terms, this represented the combined arms of the old De Kighley and Cavendish families. The Kighleys had been local Lords of the Manor for sixteen generations, had obtained the Market Charter in 1305 and sent representatives to Medieval French and Scottish wars, to claim an arguable lustre in Shakespeare's 'Sir Richard Ketley' of the death-roll at Agincourt. Sixteenth-century Anne Keighley, daughter of the last male of the line, had married William Cavendish, from whom descended the large landowning Dukes of Devonshire. The Keighleys contributed the shield's black fesse (the horizontal band) and silver ground, together with the red dragon's head of the crest; from the Cavendish side came the three stags' heads and the serpent twined round the dragon's head and facing the same way in token of marital friendship. The Cavendish fountain or circle with its wavy lines also represented Keighley's industrial water-power; the shield's blue crenellated border signified antiquity. The punning motto was laboriously explained as recognising 'the geographical situation of the town on the banks of the Worth' as well as presenting 'a moral challenge to the citizens that they should justify themselves "By Worth".'

The new Town Council wrought no immediate change, rather continued naturally where the Local Board had left off, its early meetings discussing the minutiae of local affairs. The Medical Officer reported 75 births and 43 deaths for November of 1882, together with seven cases of lead-poisoning, and recommended 'at great length' the use of charcoal filters. The Midland Railway Company requested permission to widen the Worth Valley line, and were refused. A question of giving the Assistant Surveyor three months' notice 'was referred to the Highways Committee'. Electric alarm-bells were to connect the Police Station with the Fire Brigade; attention was called to the dangerous condition of several chimneys and the 'bad state' of Lawkholme Lane, a Veterinary Inspector appointed, designs for a mayoral chain ('the handsomest chain in England') pored over. The Mayor 'made arrangements for the members to have a cup of tea if they would meet half an hour before each ordinary meeting'.

But steadily, through the eighties and nineties and as the century turned, the narrow hotch-potch town took on a more spacious air. The mighty ornamented banks went up along a widened North Street. Crushed old tavern-filled Church Street became dignified by the curve of Hattersley Crescent, whither in 1890 the Conservative Club transferred into a suite of fourteen 'lofty' rooms served by a mahogany bar (the Liberal Club, lagging again, did not acquire its 'well-appointed' Scott Street premises till 1898). A succession of mean cross-streets down Cavendish Street were replaced by smart shops, and a troublesome bottle-neck removed between the Oddfellows' Arms and the Queen's Head. Notable buildings of the period included the Bow Walk Post Office (1891), the School Board Offices (1893), the Temperance Hall (1896), the New Queen's Theatre (1900), the North Street and Low Street Arcades, the Masonic Hall, the Cycling Club ... and Prince Smith provided the town with a focal-point by raising the height of the Mechanics' Institute tower to accommodate a clock in memory of his father. Officially wound up on June 30th, 1892, its 'beautiful chimes' could be heard 'to the extreme borders of the borough'.

Chapter Eight

The later Victorians progressed to an accompaniment of new accelerating techniques. At the end of 1885 the National Telephone Company opened an exchange in Low Street (not entirely an innovation, for Oakworth House already boasted a 'telephone room' connecting Isaac Holden with his Bradford works). Mayor Edward Marriner, ceremonially 'put in communication with' his Bradford counterpart, delivered himself thus: 'On behalf of the Borough of Keighley I ask you to congratulate us on the opening of the first telephone exchange in Keighley, and we trust that this additional communication may be for the mutual benefit of both towns'. Councillors then amused themselves conversing with people in Bradford, Leeds and Sheffield, being 'much pleased with the easy way in which the different voices of the speakers could be recognised', and were regaled with cornet selections by 'two gentlemen at the Bradford office'. Dalton and Alexandra Mills were among the first to have 'wires fixed', and a public 'call office' was set up in F.W. Edwards' pharmacy.

Messrs W. and J. Bairstow took an unprecedented step in 1884 when they lit their South Street corn mill by means of electricity. The local press, in attempting to describe this latest wonder, was plunged perforce into modern technical jargon: the installation consisted of 'a Crompton-Burgin compound self-regulating dynamo-machine' – as used in the Royal Courts of Justice, the Glasgow Post Office and Birmingham Town Hall – with sixty lamps 'of twenty candle power each' distributed about the premises. Reporters inhabiting a world of gas-jets waxed especially enthusiastic over the lamps: they were 'very pleasing to the eye'; they did not blacken the ceilings, nor flicker in draughts, nor foul the air 'with the products of combustion'; what was more, no matches were needed to light them. Actually, pioneering Isaac Holden had electrically lit his winter gardens 'on the 'Brush' system' for the past couple of years; now he set about the lighting of his house, too, which predictably turned out to be 'one of the most perfect in this part of the country'. It was not, however, till 1901 that a Municipal Electricity Works were installed to meet a steadily growing public demand.

Transport within the Borough had depended on a few private omnibuses – one run by the Devonshire Hotel met 'every train at the Midland Station up to 9 p.m.' – and hackney cabs. Keighley's cabmen, exposed as they were to odd hours and the elements, became an object of solicitude in 1887 when a Hackney Carriage Committee bought them a shed. The necessary subscription list provides the customary district 'Who's Who'; whilst the pretty ornamental shelter, with window-panes of coloured glass, six seats, a stove and a wash-basin, was erected at the bottom of Albert Street and subsequently moved across to the top of Cavendish Street. In 1889, however, the larger public grew more mobile through the efforts of a Keighley Tramways Company, which laid rails between Ingrow and Utley and ran a frequent horse-tram service via South Street, Church Green, North Street and Skipton Road. Their drivers and top-deck passengers rode at the mercy of the weather; their horses went on duty with the Fire Brigade as need arose; their tracks were expensive of maintenance. In 1901, never having made a profit, the Tramways Company sold out to Keighley Corporation, which thereby became the slightly embarrassed possessor of four large and three light cars, thirty horses, and a depot and stables at Knowle Park. Three years later they electrified the system.

Official opening of Devonshire Park, 1888.

But the earlier years of the Keighley Town Council are characterised most notably by the provision of public parks. Thwaites Brow and Long Lee had made the first tentative move in this direction, when an institute reading-room of 1886 leased two adjoining acres as a recreation ground. Its only amenities were a few seats, a gravel walk and some saplings; but Edward Marriner came specially from London to open it, and his Band played, and a gala was held, albeit 'sadly interfered with' by rain. Denis Barrett, headmaster at the Trade School, proposing a vote of thanks to the Mayor, had said that 'this was the first recreation ground in the borough, but he hoped there would be many others to follow', and the next few years fulfilled anybody's wildest dreams.

In 1887 the Duke of Devonshire presented Keighley with nine acres of land 'bounded on three sides by the Devonshire Park Wesleyan Chapel, the residences of Mr Summerscales, Mr Prince Smith, junior, and Mr Henry Wright, and the precincts of Cliffe Street'. Called appropriately Devonshire Park, it witnessed an astonishing 20,000 Sunday school scholars, teachers and townsfolk celebrating the Queen's 1887 Jubilee, though not officially opened till September of 1888. Victorian parks were intended for promenading rather than playing games: hence, prominent features of Devonshire Park were its terrace commanding 'a magnificent view of the valley of the Aire, with Rombalds Moor in the distance', its bandstand and 'ornamental serpentine lake'; whilst Miss Butterfield's drinking-fountain was moved from Church Green to occupy an honourable if less traffic-congesting position about the centre. Bill o' th' Hoylus End commemorated the acquisition with naive verses which manage to convey a leisurely period flavour:

Chapter Eight

This bonny little garden
Is fine for perambulators,
Where our handsome servant-lasses
Can wheel our lovely creatures,
And oh! how happy they will be!
As time they are beguiling,
When the mammy and the daddy
Are upon the babies smiling.

The parks grew thick and fast, now. In 1891 Lund Park opened, the gift of James Lund of Malsis Hall, its highlight a 'magnificent' fountain in the middle of a pond. Eastwood House and its grounds came into the market in 1889, and was by lengthy stratagems acquired for the public good. Indeed, behind the bland surface of these benefactions lies a mesh of intrigues ('And who are they,' Bill o' th' Hoylus wrote significantly of his bonny little garden, 'who dare to say the town it did not need one?'). Briefly: the Duke of Devonshire had offered a choice of sites at Devonshire Park and Lawkholme, when Henry Isaac Butterfield of Cliffe Castle attempted persuasion to the tune of £1,000 in favour of Lawkholme; notwithstanding, the Council decided on Devonshire Park, 'without consulting the ratepayers'. James Lund had first sought to sell the Council fifty-five acres, cheap, and been refused; then to give fifteen acres, and been accepted. Henry Isaac Butterfield subscribed half the purchase cost of Eastwood Park – £5,250 – in return for the closure of Dark Lane, a troublesome right of way across his estate: a controversial negotiation which nevertheless went far to ensure the opening of the Eastwood grounds, as Victoria Park, in 1893.

Incredibly, from a complete lack of recreation space, the Corporation had assumed responsibility for three major parks in six years. One pleasant inconsequentiality was the addition to the payroll of a Lund Park pony, for pulling the mowing-machine and carting soil and peat and manure. The holder of the post in 1909 had been in rather gentle harness for ten years when 'it' – according to sexless official sources – developed 'Acute Rheumatism in its hind parts' and had to be slaughtered. 'This was done in the afternoon by David Hanson, Low Fold Farm, Long Lee. David Hanson informed us (per telephone) that he would allow us 5/- for the carcase'. An advertisement for a successor produced an engaging crop of offers: Ernest Hudson's 'Dappled Grey Pony thick set standing on short legs with plenty of nice flatt bone' (£25) ... James Feather's 'honest sound & Good worker' (£14) ... Charles Greenwood's, 'very Quite to feed and yoke' and, again, confusing as to sex: 'If you want to see him I will bring her to Keighley and let you see her yoked in any gears yow want' (£7) ... But times must change, and by 1914 the Parks Committee were antagonistically debating the cost of 'horse-keep etc.' 'More than half the pony's food up to the present has consisted of hay and grass grown in Lund Park,' pleaded the man who worked with it, 'no hay having been bought'.

Victoria Park provided the means for a further development. For years, thanks to an interest in objects natural and historical miscellaneously nurtured by local

Eastwood House, with the museum entrance on the left.

collectors, exhibitions had proved fairly safe fund-raisers in a variety of causes; like that held on behalf of the Mechanics' Institute library in 1874, which included 'Machinery in motion, Manufactures, War Implements, Moving Models and Scientific Apparatus, a large collection of Specimens of Natural History, a number of Aquaria and Ferneries, some very valuable cases of Crockery, and a numerous collection of Curiosities ... Messrs. Tom Craven, John Clough, and other gentlemen lent a large number of their Pictures. Machinery was lent by various tradesmen of the town and neighbourhood; Messrs Jesse Miller and Son, Thomas Dean and others contributed most interesting cases of Insects, Birds and Animals'. This exhibition was insured for £3,000 and guarded 'night by night' by members of the Mechanics' Institute Committee. In 1881 a Keighley Scientific and Literary Association was formed which, acquiring 'several splendid and valuable collections of natural objects', christened its Lawkholme Lane meeting-room 'The Museum'.

July 6th, 1893, saw the opening, not only of Victoria Park, but also of a Science and Art Exhibition in aid of a children's ward at the Cottage Hospital. For this purpose, the courtyard of Eastwood House (or, as it was now being called, Victoria Mansion) had been covered in to form a large hall housing another 'splendid' collection 'got together' for a four months' viewing. Both the idea and the location of a museum were thereby established, and in 1897 an enlightened Parks Committee bought some 1,700 birds, eggs, quadrupeds, bees and butterflies representing the life's work of taxidermist Jabez Bancroft, of Beechcliffe; engaged a Derby expert to mount them; and two years later were able to open a permanent Natural History Museum. Its first hundred and twenty cases of a steadily-accumulating collection were delightedly received and reported upon in detail: 'The robin has hopped down to an old chopping-block, into which the axe has been driven, and close by is a bundle of sticks. Quite a happy family appears in another case, the sheldrake, which embraces a pair of adults and five immatures. Three of the young are swimming in a small pool, and two are wandering on the sand...'

A next logical step was the provision of a public library, and the question was indeed mooted at the official museum opening. But here events took the kind of happy turn usually reserved for fairy-tales: Among the crowds at the starting of Prince Smith's memorial clock in 1892 had been the Scots-born American industrialist, Andrew Carnegie, a guest, at the time, of Isaac Holden. He had made 'a brief but stirring speech on Anglo-Saxon unity', but had never visited Keighley since. Out of the blue, then, in August, 1899, came the announcement: 'Mr Andrew Carnegie, the multi-millionaire, has offered to give £10,000 for a free library for Keighley, and the only conditions he has attached are that the town shall give a site and shall adopt the Free Libraries Act'.

The newsroom of Keighley public library in its early days – 'SILENCE'.

This was due in part to Swire Smith, now knighted, a notable Free Trader and authority on technical education. For the past quarter-century, reports, pamphlets and lectures had been flowing from his fluent pen – 'Notes on Technical Instruction', 'Municipalities and Technical Education', 'Unofficial Comments on Education at Home and Abroad', 'Technical Education in a Yorkshire Town', 'Night Schools and Technical Education' – and in the process Keighley had been publicised. 1899 found Sir Swire in a 'large and merry party' at Carnegie's Scottish residence, Skibo Castle in Sutherland, playing golf, marching round the table to bagpipes before dinner, entertained with Highland flings and sword dances, even regaling the company with comic songs. 'The fun went rather fast...' At some point, however, the conversation grew serious enough for Carnegie to ask: 'Why don't you put the Free Libraries Acts into operation at Keighley?' Sir Swire made a suitable reply ('a committee had already been appointed ... the town was heavily involved in regard to public improvements .. however desirable a free library was, it might wait a little while'). Whereupon, 'Mr Carnegie remarked, "Why, then, probably £10,000 would build a library?" Sir Swire thought that it would, whereupon Mr Carnegie at once said, "Very well, I'll give it".'

In the event, it cost £20,000, being an impressive building 'in a free treatment of Early Renaissance' and the first English library among the world-wide 2,811 materially assisted by the remarkable Carnegie. Sir Swire laid the foundation-stone in 1902, on a plot 'at the head of our newest and handsomest street' and, curiously, next to his late father's house – it was the day of Edward VII's Coronation, and a Stars and Stripes, hoisted above the ceremony in Carnegie's honour, contrasted with the bunting Union Jacks along North Street. 'A Highland crofter,' Sir Swire announced anecdotally, 'once said to me that Mr Carnegie had a heart as big as his purse'; more seriously, he envisaged the library as 'rounding off' Keighley's educational facilities, and delivered high-toned statements appropriate to the occasion: 'Some say you cannot make people happy by books, which in part is true; but to all who are intellectually inclined books are among the chief sources of happiness'. It was another two years before the library was opened by the Duke of Devonshire, ceremonially issued with the first book (he chose Grotius's *Rights of War and Peace*). The Mechanics' Institute provided both its original stock of 13,000 volumes, and its librarian, Robert Summerskill Crossley, who came 'for the time being' and stayed for forty-two years; and its news-room could seat a hundred and fifty, who drew, one hopes, inspiration from walls embellished with some of Carnegie's favourite quotations: 'They are never alone who are accompanied by noble thoughts', 'The highest truth that a man sees he must fearlessly proclaim', 'The chief glory of a nation is its authors'. Nearly 3,000 borrowed books during the first year, including seven journalists, ten policemen, two window-cleaners and 520 'married women, spinsters, juveniles, etc.' Andrew Carnegie was presented with the Freedom of the Borough.

For the Borough had entered an ebullient epoch. The Franchise and Redistribution of Seats acts of 1885 had authorised thousands of new local voters and made Keighley the centre of a separate electoral district returning its own Member of Parliament; which continued the strong Liberal tradition of the old Northern West Riding

Division in which it had previously been included. Indeed, Keighley Conservatives experienced some difficulty finding a candidate for the 1885 election, eventually persuading a young William H.C. Dunhill of Goole to stand. His opponent was Isaac Holden, now a vegetarian 78-year-old with a long political career behind him, who expectedly won 5,644 votes against Dunhill's 2,818 and went on to sit in Parliament for another ten years, dying at the age of ninety a baronet and a Keighley Freeman. He was followed as Member successively by the Liberals Sir John Brigg (1895), Sir Stanley O. Buckmaster (1911) and Sir Swire Smith (1915). Not until Conservative Unionist Robert Clough was elected to the Coalition government of 1919, was the Liberal hold on Keighley broken. 'What religion be th' master here?' a popular joke of the period put into the mouth of a stranger come to work in the town.

'A Liberal.'

'So be I. And what politics be th' master?'

'He's a Methody.'

'So be I. I be a Methody too.'

An unkind section of opinion labelled Keighley 'the city of "So be I's"' – 'and it is a well-known fact that if six long yellow chimneys were to turn blue tomorrow, there wouldn't be a Liberal in six hours in the city of "So be I's"'.

Not, by any means, that the Liberals went unopposed, for electioneering tended to be a passionate business accompanied by squibs and cartoons, bad verse and posters big enough to cover a house-side. The 'Liberal unsectarian party' published a spasmodic news-sheet, *The Electioneer*, which by 1894 was being countered by a weekly *Journal* issued by a pugnacious young Keighley branch of the Independent Labour Party eager to take on both its established opponents: 'The Difference between Liberal and Tory is pretty much that between upper and nether millstone. The quality of the two is essentially the same. They are sections of the wealth-possessing class, and on all questions affecting the Interest of Labour, They Play into One Another's Hands'. An energetic course of Labour lecturers included Keir Hardie and a dour, crippled, dedicated Cowling man called Philip Snowden, whose subject at an early meeting was characteristically 'The Religion of Socialism'. Keighley's first Labour Member of Parliament – Hastings Bertrand Lees-Smith in 1922 – lay yet in a distant future; but a first candidate put forward in 1906 won 3,102 votes, no mean score out of a total poll of 11,653.

A straightforward, unselfconscious patriotism permeated society at large. It was natural that Henry Isaac Butterfield, building a turreted outpost above Steeton in 1887, should have called it the Victoria Jubilee Tower; that the Cottage Hospital, extensively enlarged during the 1890s, should have been renamed the Keighley and District Victoria Hospital; that the Queen's death early in 1901 should have occasioned vast quantities of crepe and black-bordered editions of the local papers (although both feet remained firmly on the ground: 'As the Shopkeepers have agreed to Close their Places of Business for the Whole Day on Saturday, being the Funeral Day of our late beloved Queen,' publicly announced Mayor H.C. Longsdon, 'I shall be glad if you will Make your Purchases on Friday Evening when the Shops will Remain Open until Eleven p.m.').

23 January 1900: the local Active Service Contingent marches through the rain along North Street en route for the Boer War.

The outbreak of the South African War in 1899 was greeted with the whole-hearted formation of a Keighley and District Patriotic Fund, on the same lines as one during the Crimean War in 1855, for assisting soldiers' and sailors' families and the wounded: within one month it had raised upwards of £3,000. An 'enthusiastic send-off' was accorded to eleven Reservists recalled to the colours, five troopers of the Imperial Yeomanry, and three Ambulance Volunteers; though public excitement reached its highest pitch in January, 1900, when an Active Service Contingent of the 3rd Volunteer Battalion Duke of Wellington's (West Riding) Regiment set out for their Halifax depot, en route for South Africa. By the turn of the century, a strong military tradition had brought local Volunteer companies up to a strength of over three hundred, and the thirty-six for active service had to be selected from a willing scramble of men having 'little or nothing to gain and a great deal to lose'. Mills and workshops gave their employees time off, on a grey wet mid-day, to watch them entrain, laden with the town's gifts, pipes and tobacco, cigarettes and chocolate and socks – grocer James Groves had presented each soldier with a tablet of soap. 'Men,' said their colonel (who was not going with them), 'you are a picked body of shots, and I see from the newspapers that Lord Roberts says that one good shot is better than three bad ones. I only hope that if you have a chance you will make it a hot corner for a few Boers somewhere'. The Mayor was more concise: 'May your return be safe and speedy. May God bless you all'; and he marched with them as far as the railway station, his chain dulled by the drizzle amongst the khaki-covered helmets. Sixteen months later, a crowd of 20,000 cheered their return: in the meantime, one Volunteer, Private W.C. Emmott, from Laycock, had died of enteric fever.

In an age which bred outstanding figures, frequent conferrings of the Freedom of the Borough expressed the confidence of a progressive Council housed, from 1901, in a slightly nondescript Town Hall. John Tiplady Carrodus received the first, 'enclosed in a very lovely and appropriately ornamented silver gilt casket', in 1895. An eminent violinist born at Braithwaite, he had led the Royal Italian Opera orchestra at Covent Garden and played at most of the great Victorian music festivals: five months after being presented with his Freedom at a Mechanics' Institute concert, he died of cancer. Four more Freemen followed in 1897: two parks benefactors, James Lund and Henry Isaac Butterfield, and the past and present Members of Parliament, Sir Isaac Holden and Sir John Brigg. To the Freedom awarded to Andrew Carnegie in 1900 in recognition of his library gift, was added another to Spencer Compton, eighth Duke of Devonshire, when he came to open the building four years later. During the next decade, similar honours went to three outstanding earlier Mayors, William Clough, Benjamin Septimus Brigg and Henry Crofts Longsdon; to Sir John Clough, for his services 'in the cause of education and for the general welfare of the town and its inhabitants'; and to Sir Swire Smith.

Others, no less worthy, achieved a more modest fame. There was a bespectacled journalist with a pointed beard and an Inverness cape and wide-ranging interests in the Mission to the Deaf and Dumb, blind welfare, local history, education, phonetics: his name was Joseph Rhodes. As an early English Esperantist, he was instrumental in founding a Keighley Esperanto Society – the first in England – in 1902, and in persuading the Keighley Chamber of Commerce to become the first English body to appoint a representative to the Delegation for the Adoption of an Auxiliary International Language. His mammoth *English-Esperanto Dictionary* was published in 1908; and if its appeal is, in the nature of things, limited, the non-Esperantist can appreciate the ideals enshrined in its Dedication: 'To the English-Speaking Peoples, who, if needing less than others an auxiliary international language, may benefit most by the use of Esperanto, and by its means powerfully help forward the recognition of the Brotherhood of Mankind.'

There was a schoolmaster out at Stanbury who set his classes to planting shrubs round the schoolyard, sending exhibits to national nature study displays, digging for Roman roads. Natural history and antiquarian societies, parties of teachers, journalists, museum curators and foreign students flocked to see the work at Stanbury Board School under Jonas Bradley, whose log-book records pioneering turn-of-the-century methods: 'The snow, which has been with us for about 6 weeks, having disappeared (excepting in sheltered nooks of the moor), and spring weather and song birds come, we went out this afternoon about 2.30. There were 54 children (Standards I to VI) in charge of Mr Rushworth, Miss Simpson and myself' ... 'I took the children in two batches across to my kitchen (which I could darken more readily than any of the rooms at school) this afternoon and showed them about 120 lantern pictures of the Brontë Country' ... 'Mr Fothergill, the police Constable, had brought a live hedgehog and we watched this roll itself up, open out again and run about the yard...'

And there was another Stanbury man who made a name simply by doing what he had always done for longer than anybody else, and latterly posing for cameramen – old Timmy Feather, the last handloom weaver. His moorside cottage at Buckley Green, where his bed shared the upstairs with his loom and tubs of meal for his hens, preserved a home industry and a lifestyle older than the Industrial Revolution. In his younger days he had liked jumping and clog-dancing; porridge and oatbread formed his staple diet; he had his weekly wash on Sundays; he had been to Liverpool once and Morecambe three times. After his death at the age of eighty-five in 1910, his loom happily passed into the Keighley museum.

As those last expansive Edwardian days dwindled away, Keighley had essentially and physically entered the twentieth century. Its centre of gravity had shifted from the old High Street to a handsome new Town Hall Square on the site of an untidy Corporation stone-yard. Its 33,540 population of 1881 had become 36,176 in 1891, and 41,564 by 1901, a rise largely occasioned by a boundary extension of 1895 which brought Ingrow, Hainworth, Exley Head and Utley into the Borough. The 43,490 of the 1911 census represented a fairly stable level: later increases would be substantially due to further extensions.

Yet in some respects the early 1900s seem an age away. Traffic was still sparse enough and slow enough to allow pedestrians to stroll nonchalantly about the thoroughfares; there was a craze for walking matches, and cycling was popular. One Albert Hunter, who in 1903 cycled from Skipton to Keighley 'with his back to the front wheel of his machine' (it took him fifty minutes with the wind against him), overtook forty-five traps and carts, twenty-nine more conventional cyclists, one motor-car and two road engines. Leisurely holiday expeditions were made by wagonette and canal-barge, and the railway station rattled with trains day and night. If a necessity for keeping the tramlines clear had pushed the old horse and cattle fairs out of North Street, livestock still stood for sale twice a year in Scott Street and Russell Street and up West Lane.

The locality still yielded spells and witch charms of recent compilation, bottles filled with hair and urine hidden under floor-boards, mummified sheeps' hearts stuck full of pins and buried to ward off cattle disease. A high incidence of tape-worms gave rise to a superstitious mythology of water-wolves, little animals which moved about inside your stomach, lived on the food you ate, and slept each night with their heads on your heart. Community gossip enlarged upon the activities of exhibitionists and mental defectives to produce a sometimes laughable, sometimes pathetic folklore of quaint characters: Sidney Peacan, the hot pea-seller, stirring his

Cattle fair in Devonshire Street, c. 1900.

peas up with his wooden leg; Dicky Two-Pails trying to lift himself off the ground in two buckets, a foot in each; Old Three-Laps, jilted by his bride-to-be, lying speechless in bed at Laycock for forty-nine years…

June 28th, 1914, when an Austrian archduke was assassinated in Sarajevo, is customarily regarded as the date dividing the stable old from the traumatic new; but for Keighley the turning-point arrived slightly earlier on May 1st, 1914, when a thousand engineers came out on strike. The situation had been brewing for over a year, the men demanding another two shillings a week, the employers replying that 'the state of trade would not warrant an immediate advance'. Strikes, to be sure, were no novelty, but this one threatened a new ugliness: on its first day, two non-strikers 'were followed from work to their homes by a crowd of nearly two hundred persons, who cheered and hooted alternately, waved flags and blew horns. No violence, however, was offered'.

The next week 1,500 were idle, though some firms not associated with the adamant Masters' Federation had granted the increase. Mayor William Anderton Brigg personally dragged a belligerent striker out of an excited rabble up Albert Street ('somebody asked by what right the Mayor interfered, but his Worship replied that he was Mayor and had every right'), and the police began escorting non-strikers home through jeering men and women: one worker was hit on the eye and another found the word 'Blackleg' scrawled hugely across the end of his street. So week by week the position deteriorated: moulders and joiners also struck, and the engineers rejected a compromise offer. Workmates of a non-striking moulder from the Worth Valley Tool Works followed him all the way home to Silsden and wrecked his allotment; a tripwire ambush laid against another worker brought down and injured an 'innocent cyclist' instead. The Education Committee decided to feed deprived schoolchildren.

In such a climate, the ultimatums and mobilisation of European powers seemed of lesser importance. By July, journalists lost for words were reporting 'remarkable' scenes outside Messrs. Dean, Smith & Grace's; by which they meant the shrieking of packs of 'women of the Parkwood district', the wholesale stoning of non-strikers and police and the smashing of windows. Damage extended across the town. Fusillades assailed the frontage of the Picture House 'in which Mr H. Smith, of Dean, Smith & Grace, Ltd, has a very small interest', and for three hours a mob booed and 'sang ditties' outside Arthur Smith's Skipton Road home guarded by fifty police. When a ringleader was summonsed, a gang of 'the younger strikers' attacked the Parkside Tannery owned by one of the magistrates. Police reinforcements were drafted in, stowing their mattresses in the Drill Hall. A moulder nine weeks idle, killing time with drink, fell into the Aire and drowned. Trade Unions treated strikers' children to a picnic in Heather Glen. The branch secretary of the Amalgamated Society of Engineers received an anonymous letter from some men 'having to cease work from no fault' of their own: 'Now we, as a number, have come to this conclusion, that if this window smashing is not stopped we shall take the same game up, and let them see that two can play the game of broken pots with your windows'. The directors of the Keighley and District Mutual Plate Glass Insurance Society held an emergency meeting to search their rules and thankfully conclude that 'the form of policy issued by the Society states that the Society do not take responsibility for loss by breakage caused by civil commotion, tumult or riot'.

Then, at the beginning of August ('No Strike Settlement Yet'), local headlines took up another topic: 'War in Europe'.

Chapter Nine

The Great War – anti-German riots – recruiting and conscription – the role of women – National Shell Factory – food shortages – war hospitals – worthy causes – influenza epidemic

In 1924 Keighley Town Council commissioned the great calligrapher Edward Johnston, of Sussex, to write and illuminate a Borough Roll of Honour in memory of those who 'at the call of King and Country, left all that was dear to them, endured hardness, faced danger, and finally passed out of the sight of men'. Bound by the notable Douglas Bennett Cockerell, this consisted of '20 pieces making 40 leaves that is 80 pages of Vellum': it contained more than nine hundred names.

> 'Adams, John Edward, Acting Corporal, 27th Northumberland Fusiliers…
> 'Broster, Robert Buck, Captain, 1/4th Duke of Wellington's (W.R.) Regiment…
> 'Cooper, Wilson, Company Sergeant-Major, 10th Durham Light Infantry…
> 'Dagostino, Carmine, 22 Reparto D'Assalto, 1 Divisione D'Assalto…'

They had gone from all walks of life, from houses in rows and terraces and detached. Mere boys had enlisted, and men approaching middle age, some together in the comradeship of the Duke of Wellington's, others alone in unfamiliar units.

> 'Finan, Michael, Private, Royal Munster Fusiliers…
> 'Hinchliffe, Arthur, M.M., Lance-Corporal, Machine Gun Corps…
> 'Laycock, George, Leading Stoker, HMS *Falcon*…
> 'Parrish, Charlie B., Private, Royal Army Medical Corps…'

They ring an inescapable knell through any assessment of Keighley (as of anywhere else) during those terrible years of 1914 to 1918. As Edward Johnston observed, signing his work: 'Had more time been available, it might have been better done, tho' Time itself might not do justice to the Names inscribed'.

> 'Scott, Ernest, Private, Royal Marine Light Infantry...
> 'Shuttleworth, Harry, Air Mechanic, Royal Flying Corps...
> 'Smith, W. H. Driver, Bombardier, Royal Field Artillery...
> 'Wiles, Richard, Lance-Corporal, Scottish Rifles...'

Yet it would be an over-simplification to view the Great War in terms solely of its prodigal courage and self-sacrifice. Britain's declaration of war on Germany on August 4th 1914, came as a now inconceivably profound shock to a society unruffled for generations save by the distant murmur of imperial campaigns. Local Volunteer companies had flourished on a diet of cup competitions and dressy church parades, annual shoots and camps regarded as rather a lark: 'Dear old One-eyes,' a young blood had written to an absent fellow-officer from 'the Huddersfield Inspection' in 1895, enclosing a mess-bill receipt and news of 'the Brigade girl, who inquired very lovingly after you. I was speaking to one of my men about her, and he had the cheek to say that it was not known what the officers did with her during the day but he knew what the men did with her at night'. In half a century of weekend soldiering, the Boer War alone had tapped the spirit beyond the façade.

Now, on the opening day of hostilities, 250 Keighley Territorials – 'fine strapping fellows the majority of them' – reported to the Drill Hall (where strike police moved their kit out of the way to the sides of the room), and ten thousand townspeople cheered them off on the first stage of what would prove a very long journey indeed. Recruiting began immediately and briskly. The Ambulance Corps readied itself for service; the Mayor set up a War Relief Committee; the engineers' strike was quickly settled.

An atmosphere of strained excitement veered at times towards panic. Fear of famine initially sent housewives scurrying to buy up foodstuffs 'in a way,' one grocer commented, 'that suggested a six months' siege'. Prices rose; shopkeepers introduced their own rough-and-ready rationing; people went 'from one shop to another, getting a few pounds of flour here and a few there'. A spy mania developed: rumour enlarged on a mysterious man disguised as a woman bicycling about the district enquiring as to the location of reservoirs, and a motley guard of policemen, Boy Scouts and Water Committee employees stood nightly watch at Watersheddles and Black Hill. Eight Keighley residents of German origin were arrested on August 8th and apologetically released on August 9th. Emotions flared nastily over the last weekend of the month, when a crowd of several thousands ran berserk in the High Street and Church Green, stoning, looting and attempting to burn shops belonging to completely respectable butchers with German names – Andrassy, Hofmann, Stein and Schulz. Extra police were rushed in from as far afield as Cleckheaton; bricks and bottles flew; the Revd Father Joseph Francis Russell of St Anne's, who carried considerable weight with the Irish, quietened the situation but temporarily. It transpired, too, that the engineers' strike, though settled, was not forgotten: rioters poured up Spring Gardens Lane to attack Sir Prince Smith's home, from the gates of which police launched a baton charge wherein, according to one Mrs Jones who considered herself an innocent sightseer, 'striking out blindly, people fell in lumps'.

AIR RAIDS WARNING

KEIGHLEY CORPORATION GAS SUPPLY.

In the event of the GAS SUPPLY being CUT OFF by order of the Military Authorities, consumers are WARNED that they

SHOULD IMMEDIATELY TURN OFF THE GAS AT THE METER AND CLOSE ALL TAPS.

Until further notice NO LIGHTS SHOULD BE LEFT BURNING ALL NIGHT, except where absolutely necessary and under observation.

In the event of the Gas Supply being cut off during the night it will be turned on again at FIVE-THIRTY O'CLOCK ON THE FOLLOWING MORNING.

By Order,
W. BAILLIE,
Gas Engineer and Manager.

Gas Offices,
Keighley, October 6th. 1916.

Billows & Co., Printers and Bookbinders, 16, High St., Keighley. Tel. 224.

1916, and the Keighley Corporation Gas Supply prepares for the possibility of air raids.

A believable official version credits the police with 'the most exemplary patience during the whole proceedings'. Five ringleaders were jailed.

Indeed, for reasons of morale and security throughout the next four years and more of war, the public was of necessity handled with increasing care. *Keighley News* reporter Herbert Arthur France compiled scrapbooks of the confidential communiqués issued to newspapers: 'The Admiralty request that the Press will not publish any statements from survivors of ships or transports which have been attacked or sunk by enemy shellfire' … 'No person shall without lawful authority collect, record, publish or communicate, or attempt to elicit, any information with respect to the movement, numbers, description, condition, or disposition of any of the forces, ships, or disposition of his Majesty's Allies' … 'The following information is not to be published: Locality; indications of route taken by enemy aircraft; information as to places where bombs were actually dropped; attacks on or damage to naval or military establishments, munition works, factories, railways, docks, or shipping…'

Hence, when British airships were routed across-country by means of the Aire valley, the local populace was not informed but, seeing shapes and hearing sounds in the night sky, went in exaggerated dread of German Zeppelins. 'We do not know what is going to happen next,' stresses a worried postcard of 1916, 'we are all dark at night in Silsden'. Even Mayor William Anderton Brigg felt concerned, and wrote to the War Office vainly requesting 'one or two Anti Aircraft Guns' to protect the town.

The Great War brought many social changes. Year after year, manpower drained away into the forces. To begin with, one's patriotism and sense of adventure were ingenuously appealed to. 'Keighley Lads, Play the Game!' cried an early recruiting poster for the 2nd Bradford Pals' Battalion (Full-back: Lord Kitchener; Three-quarter backs: General French, Admiral Jellicoe, Lord Fisher and General Smith-Dorrien); 'Wanted At Once, Dashing Forwards for the Keighley Company!' 'Yorkshire,' declaimed the 6th Reserve Battalion of the Duke of Wellington's Regiment, 'with its broad acres, dense population and strapping sons, must not lag behind in this life and death struggle against the German military despot'. Recruiting meetings thronged the Town Hall Square; Victoria Cross winners came to speak, together with Horatio Bottomley, editor of *John Bull* and swindler extraordinary; drums and bugles of military bands stirred the blood; an All Saints' Bible Class and their curate marched in a body to enlist. But patriotism alone could not indefinitely meet ever-growing demands for men, and adventure lost its glamour. A new poster made its appearance headed 'The Military Service Act, 1916' – single men aged eighteen to forty-one were 'deemed to be enlisted' and could expect to be called up.

Conscription, a new concept in Britain, was not accepted cheerfully, and loopholes occasioned by bureaucratic inexperience were plugged by a rather haphazard stratagem known as 'rounding-up'. It speaks volumes for entertainment trends of 1916 that the authorities' first Keighley 'round-up' took place at the Cosy Corner Picture House, where a 'two-act drama of the slums' called *Little Marie* was raided and its male audience of military age examined. This operation netted 150 men who 'had not their papers with them', most of whom turned out to be, not shirkers, but exempted munitions workers not yet accustomed to the wartime need for carrying their documentation about with them. A Military Service Tribunal, kept busy considering conscientious objections and deferrments, surprisingly managed to preserve a sense of humour: a September applicant 'who had been given temporary exemption said he did not understand that he had got to make arrangements for the closing of his business'.

'Canon Russell: Supposing we gave you some time, could you make arrangements?
'The Applicant: Probably.
'Canon Russell: In what time – six weeks or six months?
'The Applicant: Six months would be best. (Laughter.)
'Canon Russell: Wouldn't the end of the war be better?
'The Applicant: Much. (Laughter.)
'Exemption was granted until October 1.'

Eventually, however, the hollowest jocularity wore thin. By 1918 conscription had become a subject of bitter recrimination, as some sections of public opinion made vociferous demands for (in the jargon of the day) a 'comb-out' of men exempted, by the nature of their jobs, from 'doing their bit' – this at a time when the *Keighley News* was publishing, by the dozen, week by week, photographs of 'local heroes' killed, wounded, prisoners and missing. Week by week, too, Sharps of South Street took the adjoining columns for a piece of invidious advertising: 'Ensure his safety,' cajoled the legend beside a picture of a soldier wearing a padded vest, 'by immediately soliciting an order for a "Chemico" Fabric Body Shield, which has proved to be a real life-saver'.

Meanwhile, taking men's places, women emerged to play that part in the working world which would win them the vote in 1918. At Keighley, where female labour had supported the factory system for generations, this changing role came naturally to many, but now appeals were also made to 'women who do not usually do paid work'. In spring of 1915 the Mayor, backed by such stalwarts of the community as Sir Swire Smith, F.W.L. Butterfield and Robert Clough, called a crowded meeting to discuss 'the scope of new occupations'. These were extensive, in munitions works and on farms, in shops and offices, hospitals, banks and public transport. 'In textile mills,' a Board of Trade lecturer ventured, 'there were some men employed as overlookers who might be employed in heavy engineering shops, and the women thus allowed to do a little overlooking for a change'. Whereupon the many women present indulged in 'loud laughter'.

So steadily they entered new fields. Keighley Post Office, coping with extra business despite the loss of a score of its staff in the first war year, experimentally took on a postwoman and two girl telegraph messengers, with 'satisfactory results'. In April, 1916, the Corporation Tramways engaged six conductresses, and in November began training women drivers, the latter a bold step at the risk of men's strike action – a local official of the Tramway and Vehicle Workers' Union viewed with misgiving the prospect of all-women crews working trams along deteriorated tracks with reduced street lighting. In the event, they commenced their duties under the worst weather conditions, in sleet and snow, when, out of deference to the supposedly more delicate female constitution, a drivers' protective screen was 'very cheaply' fitted up. It was symbolic of a growing spirit of emancipation that, within a week, the 'lady drivers' had replaced their affected title with 'women drivers' – 'as witness the letter "W" prefixed to the numbers on their collars'. Munitions work especially demanded labour on a spectacular scale; and before shell-making had even begun in Keighley, whilst the first male turners were still being instructed and machinery set up, some five hundred women had applied for jobs, some 'under a sense of patriotism'.

The Great War wrought drastic alterations in Keighley's industry. In 1915 its engineering firms were substantially switched to munitions centred upon a National Shell Factory in Dalton Lane. Harry Smith, chairman of a Keighley and District War Munitions Committee, scoured the locality with Prince Smith, Richard Hattersley Smith and John Stell in a search for lathes; a workforce of girls

Keighley National Shell Factory in 1915, training its first women munitions workers.

and women under male foremen aimed at an output of 5,000 high-explosive shells per week. By the Armistice they had manufactured 714,000 costing 8s 6d each. 'The Keighley shell factory,' Harry Smith (knighted for his services) would be able to say, 'turned out more shells than would have won the battle of Waterloo'. Robert Clough's Keighley Gas and Oil Engine Company gained a slender notoriety by powering the searchlight that located the first Zeppelin shot down over England. Laundry machine manufacturers geared their plants to the production of field kitchens and disinfectors; textile mills poured out khaki and flannel. Everywhere, industry boomed, wartime conditions pushing wages phenomenally upward. Turners' and fitters' approximate weekly 41s of 1914 had become 88s by 1920; builders' 10d an hour had rocketed to 2s 4d. Of course, prices followed the same trend: 'I have started,' a teenage worker noted early in 1915, 'to pay my mother 10 shillings instead of nine shillings a week owing to the food wich as gon up terribly'. A pound of streaky bacon, 11½d in 1914, cost 2s 3d in 1918; a pot of jam went up from 4½d to 1s, a bar of soap from 2d to 10d. A three-guinea overcoat at the outbreak of war was worth £7 by its close.

Gradually the town acquired a pinched look. Tram services were cut. Enterprising commercial vehicle owners tried to beat a petrol shortage by running on coal gas, necessitating enormous containers mounted overhead or towed behind. The Lund Park and Devonshire Park flower-beds were replaced by potatoes, cauliflowers and cabbages; part of the golf links was under oats. The Trade School boys dug up their football field, and classes were given outdoor lessons on wild edible greenstuffs. A strenuous allotment scheme boasted over 1,500 plots by spring, 1918.

Food supply became an ever-increasing problem. Some rather nebulous rationing 'recommendations' were replaced by sterner measures, with a paraphernalia of margarine cards, sugar tickets and meat cards, only towards the latter stages of the war, but earlier circumstances were seldom less than critical. 'The shortage of food supplies,' warned a confidential directive from the Official Press Bureau to the *Keighley News* at the beginning of 1918, 'is leading to trouble and in some cases to raids on shops. Exaggeration, or even over-zeal, in reporting such cases might easily lead to, or extend the area of, food riots'. In such a climate, the public was subjected to massive propaganda. The King issued a Proclamation exhorting heads of households to reduce bread consumption, and people were encouraged to wear a purple ribbon as a token of frugality. 'We must all eat less food,' stressed the Ministry of Food, 'especially we must all eat less bread and none of it must be wasted. The enemy is trying to take away our daily bread. He is sinking our wheat ships. If he succeeds in starving us our soldiers will have died in vain'. Children were showered with 'Mr Slice o' Bread' leaflets – 'I am a Slice of Bread. I measure three inches by two-and-a-half, and my thickness is half an-inch. My weight is exactly an ounce. I am wasted once a day by 48,000,000 people of Britain … When you throw me away or waste me you are adding twenty submarines to the German Navy'.

In 1917 Keighley achieved morale-boosting national headlines through the efforts of its Food Control Committee consisting, in the words of the *Daily Mail*, of 'headmasters and headmistresses, the officials of the Household Economy Sub-Committee, the local trades presidents, the most strenuous Socialists in the town, representatives of the farmers' associations, who are very keen on the business, and some of the wealthiest inhabitants'; which variegated body directed its special attention to saving bread. Housewives were invited to indoor and outdoor lectures and cookery demonstrations with titles like 'How to Provide Dinners at 4d to 6d.' Bread recipes using oatmeal, pearl barley, rice and maize were widely publicised; thousands of little sample ersatz loaves were distributed in the schools, where children were taught to chorus songs such as 'Each Loaf Saved Drives a Big, Long Nail' and 'Wear the Purple Ribbon'. The Keighley and District Sunday School Union appealed to boys and girls to help their country 'by not being greedy' and 'by not eating between meals'. Even the workhouse inmates were treated for a fortnight to a trial diet of porridge and pease pudding. A shop-window in North Street (a photograph of which would appear in multi-volume Great War histories) displayed an ideal one day's rations for one man. Inevitably, there grew the story of a visitor from Barnsley surveying its contents, six small sausages, half a loaf, and half a saucer of sugar: 'By gum,' he said, 'we eat as much as that at Barnsley while

Margarine queue outside the Keighley Co-operative Society's Brunswick Street store, 1917.

we're waiting for dinner. If that's what they're doing at Keighley I'm off home by the next train!' 'No community,' trumpeted the *Daily Dispatch*, 'has exhibited so much push and go in dealing with the problems of the hour ...' 'In Keighley it is said,' more soberly observed *The Times*, 'that by effective organisation the average consumption of the whole population has been brought down well below the standard...'

War affected all modes of life. The local corps of the St John Ambulance Brigade equipped Spencer Street Congregational Sunday School as an auxiliary hospital, and received its first thirty wounded soldiers in May, 1915. Later that year a section of Victoria Hospital was taken over by the military, eventually extending into Highfield Senior and Infant Schools. Morton Banks Fever Hospital followed suit in 1916, the Fell Lane Workhouse Infirmary in 1917. The arrival of a hospital train – seventy-three came during the course of the War: one batch of 200 men reached Keighley at the height of a blizzard – is vividly recreated in a near-contemporary account (its hyper-fervid style is typical of the period):

> On the arrival at Southampton or Dover of a Red Cross Ambulance Ship the DMS. Embarkation, i.e., the Officer in charge, sends to the Central Hospital concerned a first wire: – 'Prepare to receive convoy.' Some two hours later a second wire is despatched giving number of cases and time of departure.
>
> Half an hour before the train is due, Sir Harry Smith, electric torch in hand, marshals his fleet of motor cars and ambulances, second to none in the country. By-and-bye the tramp of unarmed but disciplined men heralds the arrival of stretcher bearers and 'Specials'. Needless to explain the number of cars and men bears a definite relation to the size and character of the convoy to be dealt with. On the Worth Valley platform there soon appears a solemn but suggestive array of, say, 50 stretchers ready prepared by the bearers for the broken and suffering, yet we hope, patient and happy defenders of their country's honour...
>
> First come the sitting cases, i.e., those able to walk, and a pitiable sight they are. Well may one ask: 'Are these the victors of the Marne and the Somme?' Judge not by the haggard face, the torn and mud-daubed uniform. Rather note the steady eye, the dauntless, almost reckless gait, and that despite the bandaged head, the armless sleeve, or crippled leg. God! how grand they are. . . . Half way up the station slope this maimed and motley queue received a kindly greeting and a packet of Gold Flake from Mrs Scatterty and Mr Tom Crabtree, the smokes being largely the gift of the latter. Over a million 'Cigs.' were thus dispensed, and the grateful 'Thank you, lady,' 'Thank you, sir,' are a lasting recompense for the many weary vigils and generous actions of these tireless Samaritans...
>
> Following the sitters came the stretcher cases borne by ambulance men and supported at either side by two Special Police. Arrived at the top, the cases were sorted by Majors Dobie and Crocker, assisted by the local secretary, Mr Sam Scott, into 'medical' and 'surgical', so as to facilitate transport to their respective wards. Then lifted by specially tall and stalwart 'loaders', the stretchers were fixed in the motor-vans...

Obviously, this routine depended largely on voluntary drivers, bearers and constables, but Keighley's hospital contribution did not end there, nor with its nurses, its ladies' Surgical Supply Depot nor its Wounded Soldiers Comforts Committee, for the community also entertained convalescents. Woodwork and embroidery teachers provided occupational therapy. An orchestra formed. Concert parties presented, as it were, with a captive audience, enjoyed a sort of field-day. Rowing-boats from Whitby and a motor launch from Windermere were put to use on the Leeds and Liverpool Canal. Two thousand books collected for a library at Morton Banks included a variety of classics and popular fiction, together with less happy titles like *Pretty Polly Pennington* and *The Boys' Own Annual* for 1883. The hospital chaplain had to admit that Church parades were 'not so uniformly well attended as might have been', but was nevertheless able to gather subscriptions for a chapel hopefully accommodating 250. Staff and patients even produced their own magazine, *War Hospital Echoes*, full of jokes and unbearably poignant:

> LADY VISITOR (to soldier): Well, my good man, I am sorry to see you have lost a leg.
> SOLDIER: Yes, madam, but I wish it had been the other one, as that is the one with the rheumatics in it.'

Poster advertising one of many Patriotic Concerts in aid of war funds – this one was in 1915.

Schoolchildren held little parties for men in convalescent blue; sixty were driven out to Stanbury ('fifteen motor cars in the village caused quite a sensation') for tea with the ever-hospitable Jonas Bradley and his classes.

Nowhere, indeed, is the community's quickened tempo more apparent than in school log-books: 'Standards V & VI have today visited the Morton Banks Military Hospital & carried generous gifts to our wounded heroes' … 'The girls are assisting in the making of sand-bags, by taking work home, and doing it in the evenings. Captain Wood has also asked us to make grenade bags' … 'It was decided to teach patriotic songs of Britain, France, Russia, and (if possible) Belgium' … 'Mrs Bannister absent owing to her husband's death in the Military Hospital' … 'The girls have finished the 30 pairs of socks for their fathers who are fighting in France' … 'This morning all the scholars were assembled together in the hail to have a talk about Miss Edith Cavell, as a memorial service was being held at noon in St Paul's Cathedral' ... 'Each class is visiting the Mansion House this week to see the Official War Pictures'.

It was a time of teeming activity, of myriad committees and worthy causes, flag-days and charity concerts, of mines and aeroplanes and captured German guns exhibited in the Town Hall Square. Several groups of Belgian refugees invited to Keighley in the first months of war (they were welcomed by Boy Scouts drilled to shout 'Vive La Belgique!' and by a free Picture House showing of the Biblical classic, *The Sign of the Cross*, with 'specially selected music by an augmented orchestra') stayed for the duration; the *Keighley News* featured a summary of events in Flemish. After collecting £234 18s 7d towards an Anglo-Russian Hospital in Petrograd in 1916, the town had a bed named after it, and sent out a sycamore panel carved with the coat of arms and inscription: 'To the Brave Sons of Holy Russia: Greeting and Thanks from the Borough of Keighley' (overtaken by the Revolution, this disappeared). Lonely boys in uniform wrote home to their ministers, to the *Keighley News*, to the Mayor, to their former employers: James Ickringill, worsted spinner and founder of the Oakworth Road Primitive Methodist Mission, received nearly three hundred letters beginning 'Dear Mr James' and saying things like 'you will be surprised at hearing from one of your old Good Lads' Brigade' and 'the above is my address if you care to write back'. He had them all typed and 'placed in an album, every leaf of which has been tastefully decorated, and bound in red morocco at a cost of nearly eight pounds'.

Extra burdens found shoulders ready for them. It seems hardly fair to particularise examples; but wartime conditions multiplied a hundredfold demands on the Mayor. William Anderton Brigg would modestly assert that he had been 'thrown into' public service by being made Mayor – a sporty, bachelor, travel-loving fifty-year-old – at a single day's notice in 1912. He held the responsibility till 1916. No detail was too small for him. There survives a mountain of his correspondence on behalf of individual townspeople for whom he took unending pains: requesting a day's leave for a sapper who had got a girl into trouble ('she is of a respectable family') ... advising two brothers not to join the same Battalion ('for if anything serious happened, there might be two of you involved instead of one') ... getting a soldier discharged to nurse a father whose infirmities 'are very troublesome, especially at nights, and such as strangers cannot be called in to deal with' ... enquiring as to the whereabouts of a missing lance-corporal (the answer came by way of the German Red Cross and the American Embassy in Berlin) ... 'Allow me,' wrote a signaller wounded in France, 'to offer my sincere congratulations on your accepting office for the fourth year in succession. Keighley has cause to congratulate itself on having so worthy a gentleman to occupy the onerous position at such a critical period'.

He was succeeded in 1916 by Frederick William Louis Butterfield, of Cliffe Castle, a sometime barrister of literary and musical bent and distinguished presence, on whom devolved the royal visit of May 29th, 1918. Actually, King George V and Queen Mary were in Keighley for barely one hour, into which they crammed tours of Burlington Shed and Grove Mills and a reception at the Municipal Hall, where the Queen spoke briefly among the dignitaries to Mrs Matilda Walsh, 'a widow who has had three of her four sons killed in the war, the fourth lying seriously ill from wounds in France'.

Peace, when it eventually came that November, was almost an anti-climax. Nobody worked on Armistice afternoon, and the Town Hall Square was illuminated that night, but the prevailing climate was one of 'sober thankfulness'. Indeed, the Great War carried a cruel sting in its tail. That summer of 1918 what Medical Officer of Health William Scatterty described as a 'short and sharp' epidemic of influenza hit Keighley, proved fatal to one in June, nine in July, two in August, and was gone by September. In October, however, it came back (throughout the world an estimated ten million were dying of it) and killed forty-six; during November, sixty-three. Schools were closed and cinemas requested not to admit children, since they were especially vulnerable. A milkman and two of his family struck down together were among the first victims; and a mender who had been for a Turkish bath and who died with her mother's potato poultice round her neck (the inquest 'did not think that medical aid could have saved her'). In the week prior to the Armistice there were sixty-five interments at Keighley Cemetery: navvies had to be borrowed from the Stanbury waterworks and grave-digging carried on into the night by lantern-light. Fifteen influenza deaths in December were regarded as an 'improvement'.

Two months later the epidemic recurred for the third and last time and claimed, among others, the secretary of the Keighley and Craven Building Society, Herbert Hugill MBE, who had pushed the local War Savings movement: he died on the day he should have been guest of honour at a dinner celebrating the Borough's raising of £5 million in war loans. For several weeks, too, Riddlesden echoed to volley-firing at Morton Cemetery, over the funerals of more than forty German prisoners-of-war. They had been transferred to the Morton Banks War Hospital from an officers' internment camp at Skipton, where the influenza ran riot, the Germans having, it seems, obstinately refused to keep their windows open.

Chapter Ten

Post-war Keighley – entertainment and recreation – tracklesses and buses – General Strike and Slump – industrial and political changes – social developments – housing – Borough extensions, 1938 – Spanish Civil War – Zeppelin Hindenburg – Second World War

The Victory Medal was inscribed 'The Great War for Civilisation', and the whittling down of wartime ideals by the actualities of peace has become a hackneyed theme. For a time, though, Keighley tried to return to normal, disbanding suddenly unnecessary committees, lighting up the Mechanics' Institute clock again, welcoming home repatriated prisoners-of-war, auctioning off the contents of the National Shell Factory, closing down the military hospitals … to an accompaniment of dinners, balls and galas. July 19th, 1919, was given up entirely to celebrations, with gymnastic displays and tableaux: Wesley Place Sunday School depicted 'The Dawn of a New World' ('a figure of Peace with wings, holding a crucifix; a wounded soldier, &c., &c.'); the Fleece Mills twisters showed 'a house with Mother and Father, Daughter, and returned Son', oddly entitled 'Missing, But Remembered'; and there were Britannias and John Bulls galore. 'Distinguished townspeople' presented all the schoolchildren with pewter medals.

Everywhere, in the surrounding villages, in churches and chapels and cemeteries, subscriptions poured into an eloquence of plaques, cenotaphs, statues, windows, institutes. Late in 1924 Edward Johnston's Roll of Honour went on permanent display in the Reference Library, in a glass case made specially to hold it, a fresh page turned over each day. The Keighley War Memorial replaced a clump of shrubs in the Town Hall Square (a suggestion as to siting it on Rivock had been opposed by nature-lovers): its stone was quarried at Eastburn, its bronze figures sculpted by Henry C. Fehr of South Kensington, and 25,000 people watched its unveiling.

For the first time, Keighley's population was declining: its 43,490 of 1911 had become 41,921 in 1921; 40,441 by 1931. The slackening of artificial wartime conditions unsettled the engineering industry, to the especial detriment of Messrs

Summerscales Limited, laundry and general engineers since 1850. For four years they had been turning out disinfecting apparatus and shell-cases, but the Armistice caught them newly and expensively geared to a large contract for high-explosive shells – they lost £30,000 and went into voluntary liquidation early in 1920. Troubles from the interrupted summer of 1914 resumed in 1919 when moulders and coremakers embarked on an eighteen-week strike dogged by severe hardship, in the latter stages of which the more desperate were playing a street organ at the Workhouse gates, collecting for their children.

But with the gradual stabilising of world markets, business prospered again. A Keighley Official Handbook put out in 1919 contrived – albeit unashamedly biased ('Industries and Resources and Advantages for Factory Sites and Industrial Development') – to present a potentially rosy catalogue of metal founders, machinery and machine-tool makers, textile firms and manufacturers of internal combustion engines, washing machines and springs, together with a miscellanea of tanners, timber merchants, electro-platers, motor engineers and sheet-metal workers. The Technical Institute was 'flourishing', with a mechanical and electrical engineering wing opened in 1915; the Keighley Association of Engineers, which had attracted fifty members at its turn-of-the-century inception, now boasted three hundred. 'In the revival of trade that will eventually follow the end of hostilities,' predicted an advertising brochure, 'Keighley will, it is confidently anticipated, play a conspicuous part'. And so, for a while, it seemed generally to turn out; Sir Harry Smith and his brother Arthur were among the first to plunge off into the trade fairs of an apparently expansive new Europe, Australia and South Africa; order-books filled again.

A hearty spirit of amusement and entertainment gripped the populace. The Queen's Theatre, now more commonly called The Hippodrome, was performing twice nightly to a formula scarcely intended to stretch the intellect: its programmes through 1920 billed no fewer than thirty weeks of variety turns and eleven of revues and musical comedies; four out of six plays were comedies, whilst occasional treats took the form of pantomimes and, at a slightly more cultural level, the Keighley Amateur Operatic and Dramatic Society's presentation of the comic opera *Tom Jones*. The cinema had entered its heyday, presenting a bewildering range of attractions, three times a day and advisedly book your seats, 'for those who are fond – and who is not? – of moving pictures' at the Cosy Corner, the Regent, the Oxford Hall, the Picture House, the Cavendish Street Palace, the Russell Street and the Market Street Theatre de Luxe ... When the Ideal Film Company came to make *Wuthering Heights* at Haworth, interested picturegoers trekked out for behind-the-scenes glimpses of cameramen hugging their tripods in the moorland wind and the producer wading up the Sladen Beck with child stars on his back. Sports assumed their disproportionate importance in the scheme of things, and were widely played, Association Football in particular fielding numbers of enthusiastic teams with colourful names like the Keighley Munition Workers, the Gaelic Juniors, the Ingrow Celtic and the Silsden White Star. Men's clubs clicked with a never-ending round of billiards League tournaments.

Chapter Ten

Life was being revolutionised by the internal combustion engine. Slowly but surely the owners of automobiles and motorcycles were increasing; and now anybody with a few shillings could travel, by means of the charabanc which, those first few summers after the Great War, became the overwhelming craze. Passengers universally clad in cloth caps and big hats rode companionably six to a seat, at modest speeds beneath the open skies or doubtful shelter of the folding canvas hood, bouncing on solid tyres and putting their trust in a new breed of youngish men who had learnt their driving in Army lorries. A sudden burgeoning of local proprietors fought for the custom of the day-tripping public: from their Chapel Lane garages, the Keighley Brothers and the Premier Transport Company drove out for Blackpool and Morecambe, Southport and Windermere, or Harrogate and Knaresborough for the half-day; Anderton Brothers ran more cautiously to Burnsall and Grassington; George Ashwell specialised in choir and works outings. Haulage contractors Craven and Wood invested in a 'reliable "Leyland"'; Ratcliffe & Co. of Haworth boasted the latest luxury model christened *The Pride of the Valley* – till Airedale Garages surpassed them with their half-size fourteen-seater *Lion* advertising 'pneumatic tyres all round'. It was all rather carefree, and received a momentary shock in October, 1920, when Oxenhope acquired the gruesome distinction of the first serious charabanc accident: the brakes failed in a Maudsley carrying thirty-two knur-and-spell supporters from Pecket Well to a match at Laneshaw Bridge; which ran out of control down Cockhill and smashed through a wall above Oxenhope Church. Five were killed.

Keighley Corporation Tramways had been haphazardly experimenting with motor-buses since 1908. In 1913 they had inaugurated a service of Austrian Cedes-Stoll trackless cars to some of the outer villages which, difficult of maintenance during the War, resulted in a remorseless series of deficits. Trams, on the other hand, remained viable longer, but were now faced with competition from private firms. The Premier Transport Company, on being refused permission to run charabancs along a Corporation route, had written arrogantly back: 'In reply to your letter, we note your refusal to give your permission to run, but we may tell you that you cannot give that refusal. We shall put our chars-a-banc on the road. We only asked you out of courtesy. Now you refuse it, we shall put them on the road and enter into competition with you'. The track had decayed; debts mounted. In 1924 – the first case of its kind in Britain – Keighley's entire tramways system was abandoned and replaced by tracklesses. These were supplemented the following year by a fleet of motor-buses, at last showing a surplus on the balance-sheets and destined in turn to supersede them in 1932. All of which activity affected other modes of transport. 'Horses,' commented an observer in 1935, 'are now so rare in Keighley that only a handful of shoe-smiths can make a living'; the canal was 'rarely used', and 'even' the railways were hard-hit – 'the Worth Valley Service has been curtailed so severely that the Bill-Posting Company has abandoned some of the hoardings erected along the route'.

This running-down was in part a reflection of a depressed age, for the post-war boom had flashed in the pan, after all. The advancing 1920s brought slump and

Keighley corporation Tramways car No.12 at Cliffe castle gates, 1906.

unemployment. Political and industrial unrest reached deadlock in the General Strike of May, 1926: trains and Corporation buses ceased; kindlier motorists displayed cards saying 'Signal for a Lift'. The *Keighley News* just managed to produce itself 'under greater difficulties than any issue since the establishment of the paper'. But, whilst brief duplicated *Yorkshire Observer* bulletins listed the staccato disorders of neighbouring towns – a milk train stoned at Shipley; police baton charges in Leeds; buses attacked with brickbats at Huddersfield – Keighley remained quiet, its only obvious militants some drivers and conductors of the Corporation Tramways, who went about jeering, to little avail, at the private buses which coolly took over their passengers. The Emergency Food Officer was able to assure no shortages, no panic buying, few price increases; and 'the managers of the places of amusement report that the strike has not made any difference in the numbers of their audiences'. Keighley's cinemas, indeed, carried gaily on regardless with an escapist potpourri of 'screamingly funny' comedies, 'tremendous' adventures, and dramas ranging from the 'zippy' to the 'gripping'; the Hippodrome with a nautical revue called *What Ho!*

It was a quiescence which wore increasingly thin over the next few years, as circumstances continued to deteriorate and hardship intensified. Mayor Arthur Smith started a Clog and Clothing Fund whose first Community Sing-Song in 1927 raised £40 by packing 1,500 into the Municipal Hall, which mass of indifferently responsive singers, bolstered with church choirs and the Borough Band, made their way through the inevitable *On Ilkla Moor Baht 'At* to *Land of Hope and Glory* and *Jerusalem*. The police threw Christmas parties for poor children, who each received a bag of fruit, a new penny and a toy from a Sergeant Roberts disguised as Santa Claus.

The biggest firms faltered – Dean, Smith and Grace were reduced to two or three office staff working alternate weeks. A *Keighley News* editorial saw out 1930 as 'a year of unfulfilled hopes, disappointment, and gloom', haunted by 'the spectre of unemployment and short time from first to last': at the nadir, 8,000 were idle out of a work-force of 23,000. Enquiries by a Mayor's League of Help revealed children fed wholly on fish and chips, a family with a weekly income of 9s (their rent was 8s), and a formerly successful Keighley businessman 'making his way to the workhouse at Otley'. Boys trundled home-made box-carts to the Corporation tip at Marley to spend, one of them would recall, 'an hour or two scratting about amongst the filth and rubbish to find all the unburnt bits of coal and coke and cinders, as black as the hobs of Hell'. Pawnshops played a vital role; and at Parish Feast in 1930 moneylender Oliver Preston was fatally battered about the head in his Station Buildings office by a young trolley-driver 'in desperate need of money' (that was the sensational Feast when also a gasholder exploded at Thwaites).

In 1931 the country elected a National Government led by both Conservatives and Liberals, which left the Gold Standard and began gradually weathering the crisis. For Keighley this meant a prompt reinvigoration of the textile industry, and 3,000 unemployed by Christmas represented (for the other 18,000) an improvement 'greater than the most optimistic had hoped for in so short a time'. A sad legacy would, however, be carried through the decade. 'Those who cannot find work,' a townsman wrote five years later, 'are now to be numbered in hundreds and most of those are old men, not old enough to receive the pension but considered by the masters too old to do satisfactory work'.

The very organisation of industry was undergoing drastic change, as the necessities of large-scale production swallowed old local family firms in an accelerating pattern of amalgamations and take-overs. Machine-makers Hall & Stell combined with Prince Smith & Son; the Springfield Spinning Works were absorbed by Wolsey Ltd; the Stockbridge Finishing Company disappeared into Bradford Dyers, Ltd. 'Before the War,' wrote an observer of the women's fashion-conscious 1930s, 'there were several small stocking shops, each employing one or two girls to work hand machines. Not one of them remains, but three or four large firms use power-driven machinery to make finer stockings at a lower cost, not only for Keighley but for elsewhere'. Delocalisation was affecting other areas of the community. Brewery companies took over public houses; in 1927 F.W. Woolworth & Co. Ltd ('Courtesy, Service, and Value'), opened their '3d and 6d Stores' in Low

Street; Marks and Spencer Ltd, who had run a little penny bazaar in Keighley as early as 1912, capped them in 1935 with 'easily the largest store in the town', built sadly on the site of the Fleece Hotel, described at the time as 'the most picturesque survival of eighteenth-century Keighley'. Even the Corporation Tramways – the name remained unaltered despite the demise of its trams – lost a lengthy struggle for independence and in 1932 amalgamated with the West Yorkshire Road Car Company, Ltd, itself the end product of a gobbling up of smaller concerns, including the once-mighty Premier Transport Company. Meanwhile, at the station, a bizarre situation involving two separate booking offices and staffs was resolved by the Midland Railway's assuming responsibility on behalf of the Great Northern and Worth Valley lines.

Politics grew increasingly remote, increasingly specialised in the hands of professional politicians rather than interested but essentially amateur local personalities. In the Parliamentary election of 1922, Keighley Liberal and Conservative contestants (the former being William Anderton Brigg) were defeated by an imported, seasoned Labour candidate who enjoyed a sensational 4,716 majority and a possibly less satisfying jostling across North Street on the shoulders of his 'frenzied' supporters. Hastings Bertrand Lees-Smith had sat for eight years as Member for Northampton, in which capacity he had caused a stir during the Great War by enlisting as a private in the Royal Army Medical Corps and expressing sympathy towards the pacifist views of the soldier-poet Siegfried Sassoon. He would be in and out of Parliament on Keighley's behalf till his death late in 1941 – his longest term out was 1931 to 1935 when he was temporarily eclipsed by the Conservative G.S. Harvie-Watt – and would rise to such positions as Postmaster-General, President of the Board of Education and Leader of the Opposition. Yet touchingly the locality's ultimate regard, its Freedom of the Borough and a place in its folklore, was reserved for its own son, Philip Snowden from Cowling, though he had never represented nor seriously stood for Keighley, the Parliamentary career that raised him twice to Chancellor of the Exchequer and the title 1st Viscount Snowden of Ickornshaw, being founded on other constituencies. By a further irony, Snowden was perhaps the most remote, the most difficult figure of all. 'Not for 10,000 voters,' he once said, 'will I apologise for anything I have done, or modify my attitude, or sacrifice my principles in the slightest degree'.

This between-the-wars era, so often misleadingly glimpsed in terms of stark depression on the one hand, or giddy gaiety on the other, witnessed very substantial social advances. In 1925 Keighley's 31½-acre Lower Laithe or Sladen Valley Reservoir was at last finished, capable of supplying a million gallons of water a day. 1930 saw the provision of a new Public Abattoir in Hard Ings Lane, ensuring for the first time meat 'slaughtered under the best hygienic conditions in a humane manner' – its predecessor, in ramshackle Westgate premises, whilst endearingly giving away bladders for boys to use as footballs, had also presented the degrading spectacle of beasts being somewhat casually poleaxed in plain sight. The Medical Officer of Health had long been condemning its 'inadequacy and unsuitability, from every point of view', and alternative private slaughter-houses (there had been

The Westgate slaughterhouse, discontinued in 1930.

seventeen in the Borough at the turn of the century) were generally even worse. Amongst the defects of one declared unfit were 'lighting by skylight and holes in the wall, ventilation by holes in the wall opening into a privy, drainage by a hole in the floor discharging into the beck', and pining accommodation approached through a 'common privy midden'.

The benefits of fresh air were canvassed as never before. Hiking, cycling and camping came into vogue; every year some 250 sickly children were sent for three-week holidays at the Education Committee's Humphrey Head Camp on Morecambe Bay, and in 1929 the Braithwaite Open-Air School began. The squalor of the worst nineteenth-century housing was overcome. 'New Homes for the People!' became a telling slogan (One Keighley builder thought up his own, more provoking, version: 'Houses for Heroes to Live In!') in the advertising of a new suburbia of highly desirable residences. 'Live on the Sunny Side!' cajoled the promoters of the Broomhill Estate. Another 'sunny, restful Estate' at Aireworth Park had the extra advantage of being 'one minute from Stockbridge Terminus'. On the other hand, Moorcroft Estate at Oakworth thought theirs was the 'ideal position' close to a bus route. One glossy brochure called Riddlesden 'the land of sunshine', its gardens overflowing with apples, pears and plums and its residents nightly feasting their eyes on a panorama of lights, 'especially before factory closing time'. A celebrated London doctor was quoted, doubtless to the gratification of fitter, pedestrian, pioneering Riddlesdenites: 'I envy the people who are able to walk daily from 500 feet to 1,200 feet above sea level in so short a distance. It is so beneficial to the general health, and so satisfying to the mind'.

All of which was excellent, of course, for the comfortably-off ('all you need to do is consult your Architect or Builder, and choose a site'), as it was for the working-man who enjoyed his 'skill in some form of industry', access to 'the Building Societies for which Yorkshire is famous all the world over, and a very few pounds and a good character'; but the rabbit-warren slums of Westgate and Eastwood swarmed with families lacking some – in some cases all – of the necessary qualifications. Thus began a Corporation housing enterprise with the ideal of transferring the poor out of their dark yards and ginnels on to estates where they, too, could bask in 'the maximum amount of sunshine'. After lengthy negotiations, the Brigg family sold extensive lands at Guard House – dusty official files preserve the episodes of the Inquiry Inspector who, taken to view the relevant landscape in 1923, 'said he did not want to get out of the taxi' (not surprisingly, 'no details were gone into' at that time); of Leolin Brigg and a man from the Borough Engineer's trailing about the site 'in a very heavy rain' in 1925; and of Mr Brigg's, under the circumstances rather unreasonable, 'objections to the privacy of Guard House being destroyed'. It was 1927 before some 79,144 square yards changed hands, and the following year the Corporation's first 136 houses were built at Guard House, to be supplemented by others at Broomhill, Highfield and Woodhouse.

Corporation houses stood twelve to the acre, each with a garden which tenants were hopefully expected to cultivate. By way of comparison, the King Street Club-Houses, demolished in 1937, had crammed sixty-six to an acre; out of one block of 107 dwellings, ninety-three had been back-to-back and twenty-two infested with bugs. Its death rate had been nearly double that of the town as a whole. So, happily, rows of old grey hovels were reduced to shapeless heaps of rubble, Westgate and Turkey Street, Leeds Street and the Ginnel and Eastwood Square. With them went landmarks in the folk-geography of generations: the Bay Horse Inn and the Angel, with its upper room where Keighley's early Baptists had met; the picturesque Quaker meeting-house in Mill Street; the pinfold where stray livestock had been impounded; hump-backed Quebec Bridge, scene of many a Saturday-night brawl, sturdily defying the tools of the demolition-men (in the end it had to be craned bodily into the air); the eighty-foot Corn Mill chimney alongside South Street, chipped and chiselled at for two days. Three thousand people waited for hours, to be rewarded with what the steeplejack called 'a lovely fall' – mercifully 'precisely in the anticipated direction'.

For a while, in 1933, even the fate of seventeenth-century East Riddlesden Hall hung in the balance, for it was acquired by a builder who had 'had his eye' on the estate for years and was quoted as saying: 'I cannot let sentiment interfere with business ... I must consider the valuable stone in the house and the surrounding five acres for future building development'. Whereupon, Alderman William Anderton Brigg and his brother, County Alderman J.J. Brigg, stepped briskly in, bought hall and grounds, and handed them over to the National Trust.

Aspects of the age were reflected in the town's more significant works. The steadily-increasing volume of traffic along the Bradford road led, in 1929, to the pulling down of the rather rustic double-arched eighteenth-century stone

Chapter Ten

Quebec Bridge, c. 1900.

Stockbridge, and its replacement by a sleeker, straighter bridge in ferro-concrete. An open space at Townfield Gate – possibly a relic of a Medieval common-field system – grew spasmodically to fulfil the needs of a bus terminus, though it was 1940 before a 'motor-omnibus station' proper offered protection for intending passengers. In 1936, by a stroke of near-poetic irony, a Maternity and Child Welfare Clinic took over a corner of the Westgate slum clearance area – the remainder would lie waste for the next three decades, though the Second World War could be partly blamed for that. In 1938 came an 'Art Deco' super-cinema, the Ritz, seating 1,500 and guaranteed 'absolutely fireproof', complete with a cafe open for ten and a half hours a day, a car park (sure sign of the times), and a staff of 'nearly forty' who included a resident organist Wilfrid Southworth, 'well-known to thousands of radio enthusiasts for his popular broadcasts'. Just in case any picture-goers should remain unimpressed, its promoters volunteered the information that it had been built with a million bricks.

In 1938 too – after more than eight years' debate and argument – came another, and final, extension of the Borough boundaries. This absorption of Haworth, Oxenhope and Oakworth urban districts, together with the Morton portion of a Keighley rural district which had included Steeton, Eastburn and Sutton (all three were redistributed under the Skipton Rural District Council) multiplied Keighley's area by six, from 3,900 to 23,611 acres, making it the largest non-county borough in the country. Much of this newly-acquired acreage being moorland, other statistics failed to increase on the same scale: the population rose from the 40,441 of 1931 to an estimated 58,000 – it was 56,944 at the next census in 1951; the rateable value from £263,000 to £352,000. Town Council membership grew from twenty-four to forty.

At the same time, Keighley assumed responsibilities for areas traditionally jealous of their independence. The small Haworth council had enjoyed a reputation for bellicosity and discord ('The one topic on which unanimity could be relied upon was independence and the determination that any linking-up with Keighley Borough should be evaded at all costs'); in their halcyon days, at the turn of the century, they had resisted every inducement to provide a library, including an offer of £1,500 from Andrew Carnegie. Oakworth council, whilst leading a 'steady, happy life', had been struggling with a formidable 9,125 acres and twenty-six miles of road. Oxenhope's local government had been distinguished for decades by its extreme imperturbability; all its council members had on some occasion been elected unopposed. The seven gentlemen forming the Keighley rural district council, described on its disappearance as 'quaint', had cultivated 'a tenacious adherence to individual views' in the cosy atmosphere of their comfortable little room. It is noteworthy that some Haworth councillors, in perforce retiring from public life, bought as souvenirs the chairs on which they had sat in office.

Insularity was crumbling at both local and wider levels. A Keighley branch of the International Brotherhood Alliance, formed in 1905 'to cultivate and encourage a personal and collective friendship with people of other nations', had boasted three hundred members by the eve of the Great War, and struck a rapport with suburban Paris to be commemorated in the naming of the unpronounceable Suresnes Road. Afterwards, Keighley adopted the small battle-scarred town of Poix-du-Nord and gave it a red-brick community centre known, doubtless equally unpronounceably, as the Keighley Hall. 'We, the present inhabitants of Keighley and Poix-du-Nord,' orated the French Maire at the opening ceremony in 1922, 'are united in a bond which will remain unbreakable during our lives: Vive Keighley! Vive l'Angleterre!' Between-the-wars summers tempted local parties on to the continent, several hundreds at a time – one holidaymaker in Blankenburg, seeing a sign 'Yorkshire boy behind the bar' in a hotel window, slipped inside to find a Belgian he had grown up with as a refugee in Keighley.

It was only an interlude, of course. The shape of things to come was indicated in the autumn of 1937 when the first of over a hundred Basque children evacuated from the Spanish Civil War were accommodated at the Morton Banks Sanatorium, the largest of a number of camps set up by a Yorkshire Committee for Spanish Relief whose chairman was the Revd John Nicholson Balmer of Devonshire Street Congregational Church. They had fled from a world of alien violence, frightened by the flashes of newspapermen's cameras; some of them carried what purported to be letters from their parents, but which smacked suspiciously of Communist propaganda: 'I, your father, and the fathers of the children who are with you do not kill in aggression, but defend themselves ... We are Red as the poppy, but we are Red because they have shed our blood, and our bodies are stained with the red blood which runs in our veins...' When the last of them returned home in the summer of 1939, Mr Balmer went with them as far as the International Bridge on the Spanish frontier at Hendaye, to glimpse a turmoil of refugees, Red Cross officials, nuns, and soldiers 'utterly slovenly and dirty, with old blankets for capes'. Invited to dinner with three Fascists, he remained mindful of the current trend of opinion and 'thought his own thoughts when they toasted General Franco'.

Another portent came out of the sky on May 22nd, 1936, when the German Zeppelin *Hindenburg*, en route from the United States to Frankfurt, altered course to cross Yorkshire on a line from Barrow-in-Furness to Thorne that brought her over Keighley on a fine Friday evening. She was the biggest airship ever built, 804 feet long, her size creating an illusion whereby local eye-witnesses described her as 'nearly touching the tree-tops' or 'blotting out the sky'; she was low enough for her name and number, and the swastikas on her tail, to be plainly visible, together with the faces of passengers looking out. Over the High Street she dropped a parcel containing a bunch of carnations, a small silver and jet crucifix, a picture of a flying-boat, some postage-stamps, and a sheet of *Hindenburg* notepaper:

> To the finder of this letter. Please deposit these flowers and the cross on the grave of my dear brother, Lieutenant Franz Schulte, i. Garde Regt. zu Fuss. Prisoner of War in Skipton Cemetery in Keighley near Leeds. Many thanks for your kindness, John P. Schulte, the first flying priest. N.B. Please accept the stamps and picture as a small souvenir from me. God bless you!

The German Zeppelin Hindenburg *over Westfield Crescent, Riddlesden, in 1936.*

There was no mystery about this, once the geographical ambiguity had been unravelled. Franz Schulte, one of the Skipton prisoners-of-war who had died of influenza at Morton Banks in 1919, was buried in Morton Cemetery; now his brother, Father Schulte, 'the flying priest', shortly bound for mission work in the Arctic, was a passenger aboard the *Hindenburg*. The flowers, with great ceremony and a visit from British Movietone News, were laid on the German grave, where barriers had to be erected to keep souvenir-hunters at bay; the crucifix went into St Anne's Church; and two Boy Scouts who had retrieved the parcel kept the postage stamps and flying-boat picture.

But an element of speculation remained. The precise Germans had dropped their package within yards of the Devonshire Hotel, traditional centre of Keighley; yet the many snapshots and eye-witness accounts (albeit not conclusive, since the former are largely disappointing, the latter contradictory and liable to confusion with a second *Hindenburg* appearance) suggest that the Zeppelin plotted an apparently erratic but comprehensive course over the town via Utley, Black Hill, Fell Lane, Victoria Road, the High Street, Bradford Road and Riddlesden. There is a very strong suspicion indeed that she was actually taking aerial photographs.

When war came again in 1939, this threat from the sky created immediate counter-measures. Within the first two months Keighley had air-raid shelter accommodation for 2,600. People hypothetically caught in the open during an emergency could scurry for concrete-lined trenches in the Town Hall Square, Victoria Park and the High Street roundabout ('these trenches will be found to be quite dry'), or for the timber-propped basements of the Co-op Tailoring Department in Low Street, some North Street and East Parade shops, and a row of reinforced cellars in Sun Street ('these shelters are designed to provide protection against blast and splinters, but they will not withstand a direct hit'). School classes practised excitedly filing out into the damp brick darkness of playground sanctuaries. Fire-watching parties were formed; shops and offices issued with bags of sand; an advice bureau set up in the Public Library originated with the intention of supplying information after raids. Black-out descended on the town, and a new category of law-breaker appeared in the harmless guise of the householder with a chink in his curtains. Signposts were taken down, to confuse theoretical enemy parachutists; even the word 'Keighley' was painted out of the sides of Corporation vehicles. Notwithstanding, the district was deemed safe enough to receive first an influx of children from Bradford, later evacuees from London. One of the latter was asked for her three most striking impressions of life in Keighley: 'The first was what she termed the strange custom of stringing lines of washing across the streets every Monday morning. The second was the "lackadaisical way" in which everyone, from the grocer to the pedestrian, seemed to go about his or her daily tasks, and the third, the early hour at which the public 'bus services ceased'.

Actually, the air war occasioned a good deal of local activity, though for security reasons it never got into the papers. A member of the Royal Observer Corps, from the Black Hill post, reminisces: 'We had several crashes. One at Nab End. A Mosquito from Lincoln was showing off, he had no right to be there. Anyway, he crashed and two of our crew had to go to the inquest. A wing of a Wellington broke off near Bradley – that crashed. A Whitley crashed at Silsden. Another Whitley crashed on Ilkley Moor. They thought they were over the sea because they threw out their dinghies. Another bomber crashed near Oakworth. It was a terrible night and although only a few miles away nobody heard anything on the post. A Miles Master aircraft came down on Keighley Golf Course. It was damaged – they cleverly put it on a canal boat and took it back to its base...'

The Second World War, unlike the First, implied the possibility of actual invasion: one summer Sunday morning in 1941, Keighley became the centre of a mock battle in which the Home Guard fought off numbers of Regulars masquerading as German paratroopers or disguised as enemy saboteurs. Civilians out for strolls without their gas-masks or identity cards found themselves 'inconvenienced' by tear-gas or rounded up as suspects; though they could draw solace from the fact that 'most of the attacks on public utility services were broken up and the vital points kept safe from damage'.

The pinched wartime look returned. This time public and private railings and gates were swept away – 'owners will have to accept it as a contribution to the war effort'. Canal bridges could not be strengthened to meet the weight of bigger buses (the West Yorkshire's small ones were worn-out and irreplaceable): passengers up Granby and Swine Lanes had to get out and walk across. A British Restaurant serving cheap communal dinners was opened in Marlborough Street Congregational Mission, and proved so immediately popular that works were requested to stagger their lunch hours. 'Stay-at-home' holidays were encouraged, with special attractions laid on: Keighley Parish Feast of 1942 boasted a fair and concert parties in Victoria Park, sheepdog trials in the Highfield Recreation Ground, bands and cricket matches, the National Fire Service athletic sports and a push-ball competition sponsored by the *Daily Mail*. Intellectual highlight of the week was a 'Brains Trust' whose panel included a professor, a broadcaster, a missionary, and Keighley's new Labour Member of Parliament Ivor Thomas, holder of an Oxford Double First and Blue and former sub-editor of *The Times*; the following winter his motion for the Sunday opening of theatres and music-halls would cause a national sensation. He was shouted down in the House; the Archbishop of Canterbury expressed his disapproval; and the Lord's

Keighley War Weapons Week, 1940. Mayor Joseph Denby riding through town in a whippet tank.

Day Observance Society offered up public prayers for the good of his soul ('May God deal with Ivor Thomas as He dealt with Saul of Tarsus') and the defeat of his 'God-dishonouring proposals'. Mr Thomas urbanely suggested that his critics 'read Mark 2, verses 27 and 28, Luke 13, verses 14 and 15, and John 5, verse 18'.

Again the town buzzed with worthy causes. A Keighley Stickers' Club captured something of the spirit of the War's earlier years, its only object being 'to bring civilians together and to provide them with a visible sign of their unity' in the shape of a badge costing one penny – anybody could join, so long as they determined to 'stick it' at all costs, and wear the badge. At a more practical level, a Keighley and District Spitfire-Hurricane Fund instituted during the Battle of Britain raised £10,000 in a few weeks, in recognition of which the Borough coat of arms embellished two aircraft. Slogans and drives abounded: Bombers and Bombs for Victory, War Weapons Week, Warship Week, Salute the Soldier Week, Savings Drive, Book Drive, Salvage Drive ... it is fruitless to ponder the extent of priceless material re-pulped through the latter, though the Director of Cleansing enthusiastically commented that 'people have put patriotism before antiquarian sentiment'. In an excess of extroversion, Keighley even 'adopted' a town in the Soviet Union, plumping for Yaroslavl, north of Moscow, and cabling from a mass meeting at the Ritz: 'The people of Keighley send to the people of Yaroslavl greetings...' Unfortunately, Yaroslavl had not sought an introduction and did not reciprocate, though Keighley, undaunted, paid for seven hospital beds in Stalingrad. 'We convey this gift,' said an accompanying message, in words that would have an ironic ring within a few years, 'in the confident hope that it may add one further link drawing our two great countries together in ever closer bonds of friendship and goodwill in a world our common efforts shall establish in enduring peace'.

Chapter Eleven

1945-1974 – developments and demise

Even in the midst of the war, in 1944, Keighley discussed ambitious plans for a new town centre based on five zones – civic and government administration; business and professional premises; shops; warehousing and light industry; recreation and entertainment – which would have entailed a redistribution of library, post office cinemas, theatre, bus station, market (a Town Hall was envisaged in Bridge Street); complete with an inner ring road, and a bypass from Bradford Road through East Parade to Halifax Road interestingly called Worth Way. In a Council Chamber hung with maps that emphasised 'the magnitude of the scheme', the matter was understandably and indefinitely referred back.

Indeed, the street parties and bonfires greeting the end of the Second World War in 1945, provided happy episodes in otherwise austere times. Shoppers still queued with their ration-books. The Town Clerk, bleakly reviewing Keighley's position, 'did not think the prospects were bright': the textile industry had fallen off, wartime alternatives were winding up, and he feared (needlessly, in the event) large-scale unemployment. Some factories – '73 per cent being more than sixty years old' – had deteriorated whilst being used for storing food. A housing shortage was temporarily solved only by putting up prefabricated dwellings on the Corporation's Bracken Bank and Woodhouse Estates. A sad new immigration arrived out of the European turmoil, Poles and Ukrainians, Latvians and Estonians, coldly labelled Displaced Persons or, more kindly, European Volunteer Workers. More than two hundred moved initially into Howden Hall Hostel at Silsden, twenty-five into Bracken Bank House. 'I could write a book about them,' said one involved local, 'and the title of that book would be: *Tragedy!*' They brought into the district a colourful new culture, of song and dance and bright costume that belied their recent sufferings and present hardship:

> Dear Sir! I am working at Ingrow John Haggas Ltd. My name is Wanda Sztejnke. My husband Jan Sztejnke was all the time in transit camp Market Harborough. Now, because

> we want to be together, he has come to me, and Mr Haggas promissed him employement in his firm, the onliest difficultie being lodgings. We tried to get a room but in vein, because it is very hard to get lodgings here in Keighley…

Even the weather sympathised with the atmosphere. September, 1946, witnessed possibly Keighley's worst-ever floods (the previous known record, in 1900, had been limited to Morton), with water five feet deep in parts of Stockbridge and people stranded in their bedrooms at Haworth. That winter, snows isolated villages, disrupted traffic and telephones, caused power cuts and fuel shortages. Cock Hill, Cringles and the Moss were blocked for days; a Worth Valley train steamed manfully as far as Oakworth, then stuck. Mills laid off their workers; sheep froze to death in moorland drifts.

Gradually, through mid-century, life settled into a seeming affluence, but there were no sudden miracles. The last of Keighley's old common lodging-houses, in Turkey Street, was not demolished till 1964. Its worst factory fire occurred, not in a murky Regency or Victorian past, but on February 23rd, 1956, when a man, a boy and six women died in a blaze at Eastwood Mill, a four-storey spinning premises whose timber floors were impregnated with oil. As Keighley Member of Parliament Charles R. Hobson put it, raising a question in the House: 'Not only was there no warning system whatsoever, but the fire escape did not reach all floors. The staircase which was normally used by the workers when they came out of the mill was made of wood, with the exception of the last flight of stairs – seven in number – which were made of concrete. The door at the bottom of these steps was fastened, contrary to all regulations'. The firm, Robert C. Franklin, Ltd, was fined £15. In the mundane round, squalid habits of generations died hard: in 1971, the *Keighley News* conducted a dispassionate survey reading like a latter-day Ranger: 'Passage, Black Horse to Market Place, rear of Black Horse: Litter everywhere – from dead birds to paper. Strewn with dog and cat dirt. Weeds grow … Beck Side Steps Rear of Hattersley's: The beck itself is in poor condition – littered with paper, tin cans, tyres and metal barrels … Disused Dam at Berry Lane: The rubbish is piled up 12 to 15 feet high…'

*The demolition of Keighley's old market, 1971. (*Keighley News *photograph)*

Chapter Eleven

The population stabilised, with a slight tendency to drop: the 56,944 of 1951 was 55,845 by 1961, 55,263 in 1971: though its composition underwent subtle changes as a proportion of town-dwellers moving out beyond the Borough boundaries were replaced by Pakistani and Kashmiri immigrants. Politics reached an equilibrium: when Ivor Thomas went out in a roar of controversy by turning Independent in 1948, he was succeeded, fairly predictably, by Labour Charles R. Hobson, but thereafter the pendulum swung either way – W. Marcus J. Worsley (Conservative) in 1959, his majority a mere 170; John Binns (Labour) in 1964; Miss Joan Valerie Hall (Conservative) in 1970.

In industry, the tempo of merging local firms grew faster: Prince-Smith & Stells disappeared into the vortex of Platt International Ltd in 1970; the Butler Tool Company swallowed old Elliott Mitchell Ltd in 1971; closures and amalgamations decimated the directories of former days, with little regard for the loyalties of workers too easily sentimentalised but occasionally ringing true. 'Now I realise that I am growing old,' wrote a retiring foreman of half a century's service in 1947. 'One day in 1896 while running an errand which brought me along Parson Street, I stopped to watch them load or unload a waggon at Dan Mitchell's, when old Dan spotted me and asked what are you seeking Lad a job, I answered well I haven't one, well said he I could do with a Lad like thee, alright I answered I'll tell my Father, so that is how I came to D. Mitchell's' – where he stayed for fifty-one years until 'I shall have to say goodbye, and when that Day arrives I shall say with all my heart, 'Long Live Dan Mitchells' and may everyone connected with the firm be happy and prosperous'.

Gradually, Keighley grew cleaner, a convenient carbon-copy of other towns of the later 1900s. A tidy covered Market replaced the old boisterous weather-beaten rough-and-tumble under the Parish Church. One wet May day in 1968, dignitaries under umbrellas opened a bright new shopping precinct shifting the centre of gravity away from North Street and Cavendish Street into an erstwhile dreary area north of Low Street. 'The very heart of the town,' enthused the developers, sketching incidentally the maelstrom that twentieth-century urban life had become, 'is renewed by this ideal new Shopping Centre. The precincts give shoppers complete freedom from all the unpleasantness, the noise, fume and danger of vehicular traffic and have been carefully laid out to maintain a balanced flow of pedestrians throughout the whole of this revitalised area' … there was a good deal more of this in the brochures ('interest is maintained by the partially closed vistas created by the careful alignment of the Precincts and by the differing atmospheres in different parts of the Centre'), accompanied by drawings of upright citizens with fine bronzed faces and elongated legs. In the middle stood a statue of Giant Rombald throwing a boulder, an Ilkley Moor legend rather lost on Keighley and a daring sculpture which shoppers received with comments varying from 'ridiculous' and 'awful, a monstrosity' to 'not bad' and 'quite nice'. Ventured one more imaginative middle-aged lady: 'It symbolises Yorkshire – rugged'. Be that as it may, smaller shopkeepers were snuffing out as the supermarkets moved in.

A new shopping centre takes shape: Cook Lane in 1968. (Photograph by J.S. Cardwell)

Meanwhile, housing estates sprawled ever outwards across the fields; nearer at hand, blocks of flats sprang skywards. Three at Westgate Gardens completed in 1960 replaced 101 slum dwellings, a brass foundry and a builder's yard, and they enjoyed comprehensive amenities, underfloor heating thermostatically controlled, electric wall fires, cookers, immersion heaters, wash boilers and built-in clothes dryers; though their sleek uncompromising lines jarred against the gentle hills as the old grey crooked roofs had never done.

Churches and chapels, recently filling both spiritual and social needs, disappeared or turned into warehouses with a speed that the previous generation would have found shockingly unbelievable. Solid nineteenth-century residences, too, were demolished, or converted to country clubs and old people's homes; though the Butterfields' Cliffe Castle was rescued by Sir Bracewell Smith, a former Keighley schoolteacher risen to Lord Mayor of London, who presented house and grounds to the town in 1949; only after protracted debate, controversy, further gifts, a hard battle against dry rot, and a paring of its larger-than-life turrets, did the building emerge as an art gallery and museum. Other landmarks fared less well: the Queen's Theatre somewhat nonchalantly pulled down in 1961; the Mechanics' Institute burned out after a Saturday-night dance the following winter, Prince Smith's clock stopping at five minutes to four of a bitter March morning with the fire-fighters' water freezing down the walls. For years its shell would remain, growing a not unpleasing mossy patina, awaiting wheels set in motion for a Technical College extension on its site.

Chapter Eleven

Keighley Mechanic's Institute ablaze in 1962. (Keighley News *photograph*)

Repeatedly, with accelerating communications and shrinking distances, aspects of Keighley, laboriously built up, tended instead to phase out. All the hospitals vanished in favour of a regional complex at Eastburn. Railway services diminished, the station threatened with closure. Cinemas wound up. The *Yorkshire Post* abandoned its Cavendish Street office. In April, 1974, as part of a massive national reorganisation of local government, the Borough itself ceased to exist: Keighley became simply a portion of Bradford Metropolitan District.

Chapter Twelve

Twenty-first-century Keighley

When this history first appeared in 1974, on the very eve of the absorption of the Borough of Keighley into the City of Bradford Metropolitan District, the time seemed uniquely appropriate to write a full stop to its progress. But history, of course, is a continuous and not necessarily tidy process.

The present-day reader – accustomed perhaps to a system of local government emanating from ten miles away – may well have found unexpected the preceding recital of a town forging its own affairs through the successive powers of Improvement Commissioners, Local Board of Health and Borough Council. For a while after 1974, some expressions of Keighley individuality survived in such details as a six-year bureaucratic struggle for permission to re-erect former Borough coats-of-arms at its old boundaries. But as the years passed and another generation grew up, memories of the town's former status increasingly dimmed, Bradford being blamed, rightly or wrongly, for Keighley's failings.

True, in 2002 Keighley was deemed to qualify for a new Town Council, by no means comparable with the old Borough Council although its members embraced the trappings of their predecessors. What they lacked in power they made up for in enthusiasm, regarding themselves as at least 'the loud and clear voice of Keighley people'. Indeed, Keighley's former Borough arms were displayed as never before.

But not by any stretch of the imagination can the last thirty or so years be construed as easy for Keighley. A steady roll-call of familiar names marked the closure of businesses large and small: Hattersley's North Brook Works, Ondura's Burlington Street plant, the Airedale Dyeing Company, Jonas Wells ironfounders, Bottomley's mint rock…

The preceding pages have included many comments on broad themes by means of personal impressions, and here is another. When the Prime Minister visited Peter Black's in January, 1983, she was regaled with double-edged verses by 'Black's poet laureate':

Welcome, Mrs Thatcher, to our family firm,
We're the only factory round here working full-term...

But their short-time and redundancies were to come. Nevertheless, the traditional diversity of Keighley products survived if less flamboyantly than before, ranging from beer and office furniture to military regalia, security systems and self-adhesive labels.

The population underwent radical changes. The 1981 Census totalled 57,451, the 1991 58,908, recording a cautious 8.6% Asians in the South Ward, 9.4% in the West Ward, and 20.6% in the North Ward. By the end of the twentieth century Keighley had earned a dubious reputation for 'one of the highest rates of racial incidents in West Yorkshire'. More positively, an Inter-Faith Group strove to resolve differences whilst MP Mrs Ann Cryer gamely tackled the issue of forced marriages. The Jamia mosque introduced an exciting new architecture to modest Emily Street, and Asian entrepreneurship breathed new life into the desirable residences of Hillworth Village – Keighley's former Union workhouse.

The 2001 Census (albeit conducted in a manner scarcely conducive to accurate results) gave a population total of 60,471, although, with residents increasingly identifying with outer districts, there was a tendency for town proper issues to founder. A Keighley Civic Society, unable to recruit more than a few dozen members or to attract even them to its meetings, folded up. A Keighley civic and arts centre was seriously talked about for years, then was talked about no more. The Summerscales Music Festival, once a prime date in the cultural calendar, dwindled, was resurrected, then died again. Despite outspoken protests, Victoria Park was carved up.

Late nineteenth-century Keighlians had been at legal pains to safeguard Victoria Park for 'many generations to come', but the ease with which their intentions were circumvented – the Keighley Corporation Act of 1891 having been quietly annulled ninety years later by the West Yorkshire Act – casts doubt as to the future of former principles, should changing circumstances be considered more pressing.

Yet here and there the old spirit of local enterprise made itself known. Keighley's last cinema suddenly closed down with severe structural defects in 1983, but thanks to individual initiative reopened two years later as a renovated Picture House. 'This,' observed Lord Bernard Miles on its official reopening, 'is the greatest event happening in this country tonight.' Although that venture proved short-lived, the Picture House was to reopen as a private enterprise yet again, this time with greater success.

Private initiative tastefully refurbished the defunct turn-of-the-century Royal Arcade, and the Keighley and Worth Valley Railway Preservation Society contrived, amongst its other functions, to move Foulridge station stone by stone to Ingrow. Cliffe Castle's chandeliers, sold off a generation earlier, were brought back and restored to their former glory.

And on the surface at least, the town improved. The 1960s shopping precinct, having rather faded after twenty years, was revamped as a pleasanter Airedale Centre. The Cavendish Street canopy was twice renewed, and the railway station spruced up. The controversial Aire Valley Trunk Road, opened at last in 1988, turned out to be not so environmentally ruinous after all. Sensing viable business, supermarket chains moved in, their car parks becoming a noticeable feature as seen from adjacent hills.

Morrisons, enlarging their premises in 1984, illegally demolished the Britannia Hall at six o'clock on a Sunday morning. This was a Victorian building, however run-down, which Keighley could ill afford to lose, but elsewhere were indications of sympathy with the town's past. Temple Street, declared a conservation area and returned to commercial and residential life, celebrated the completion of its refurbishment with the first of a series of annual Edwardian street fairs in 1985. This occasion doubled as the official opening of a Disabled People's Centre which made imaginative use of old premises. When in 1982 Keighley Parish Church was threatened with closure due to dry rot, more than £41,000 was raised in two years.

A growing interest in the local past gave rise to lively Family and Local History Societies. The National Trust improved East Riddlesden Hall, and the Market Cross returned almost to its traditional position in Church Green; although historical reconstruction was found to have its limits when the landscaping of the adjoining site into a semblance of Medieval sward had to be modified – a wet climate in conjunction with people taking short cuts and playing football soon reduced an originally level green to mud and water. Grassy mounds had to be created instead. It remains to be seen how yet another planned reconstructed urban green will fare, and how Friday-night roisterers will treat its proposed sculptures.

We cannot write a neat ending to Keighley as it stands in 2006, a town with ambitious dreams like a new 'space-age' £23-million college campus, and a community not without its ironies: its late Victorian Temperance Hall converted first to bingo and bars then to a Wetherspoon's public house; its Temple Street Methodist Church now a Bangladeshi mosque; and those who, after twenty years of arguing over the Aire Valley Trunk Road, realised on its completion that it offered an opportunity to view their locality from a new angle. Till the novelty wore off, people walked, jogged and rode horses along the Trunk Road.

One of a number of churches meeting the spiritual needs of a growing suburban population, St Peter's worshipped from 1872 in iron premises before consecrating this impressive building ten years later. It was demolished in 1956.

Further Reading

Almond, A.; *Biography of James Ickringill, Esquire*, Keighley, 1919.
Ashraf, Mary; *Bradford Trades Council, 1872-1972*, Bradford, 1972.

Babbage, Benjamin Herschel; *Report to the General Board of Health, on a Preliminary Inquiry into the Sewerage, Drainage, and Supply of Water, and the Sanitary Condition of the Inhabitants of the Hamlet of Haworth, in the West Riding of the County of York*, London, 1850.
Baildon, W. Paley; 'The Keighley Family', *Yorkshire Archaeological Journal, Vol. XXVII*, 1924.
Baines, Edward; *History, Directory and Gazetteer, of the County of York: Vol. 1: West Riding, Leeds*, 1823.
Bancroft, Harry, Asa Briggs and Erie Treacy; *One Hundred Years, 1848-1948*, Keighley, 1948.
Barnett, M. Ratcliff; *Sladen Valley Waterworks: Souvenir of Inauguration Ceremony, August 11th, 1925*, Keighley, 1925.
Barraclough, F.; *A Short History of Keighley Post Office*', 1941. Typescript.
Bawdwen, Revd William; *A Translation of the Record Called Domesday, so far as relates to the County of York*, Doncaster, 1809.
Bradford Illustrated Weekly Telegraph; 'A Series of Picturesque Views of Castles and Country Houses in Yorkshire', Bradford, 1885.
Brigg, John: *The Industrial Geology of Bradford*, Leeds, 1874.
Brigg, John J.; *East Riddlesden Hall*, Keighley, 1936.
Brigg, John J.; *The King's Highway in Craven*, Cross Hills, 1927.
Brigg, William Anderton, editor; *The Parish Registers of St Andrew's, Keighley*, Vols. I and II Yorkshire Parish Register Society, 1925.
Briggs, Asa: *Industry and Politics in Early Nineteenth-Century Keighley,* Bradford Antiquary. Vol. IX, New Series, 1952.
Briggs Bros. Ltd: *Riddlesden*, Silsden, *c.* 1930.
Burrow & Co.; *Keighley: its Industries and Resources and Advantages for Factory Sites and Industrial Development*, Cheltenham, 1919.
Butterfield, Sir Frederick W.L.; *My West Riding Experiences*, London, 1927.

Caldwell, T.B.; *Check List of Keighley Newspapers and Periodicals (to 1914)*', 1971. Typescript.
Carrodus, Ada; *J. T. Carrodus, Violinist: A Life Story: 1838-1895*', London, 1897.
Clevely, Hugh; *It Should Never Have Happened: a Book about Notable Fires*, London, 1957.
Cowling, Eric T.; *Rombalds Way: a Prehistory of Mid-Wharfedale*, Otley, 1946.
Craven, A.; *Commercial and General Directory of Keighley, Bingley, Skipton, and Surrounding Districts*, Keighley, 1884.
Craven, C.W.: *Victoria Park: A Record of Events Showing How it was Acquired for the Use of the Ratepayers of Keighley*, Keighley, 1893.
Craven, Joseph: *A Bronte Moorland Village and its People: a History of Stanbury*, Keighley, 1907.

Dewhirst, Ian: *Gleanings from Victorian Yorkshire*, Driffield, 1972.
Dewhirst, Ian: *The Haworth Water-Wolf, and Other Yorkshire Stories*, Driffield, 1967.
Dickens, J. Norton: *The Roman Road from Manchester to Aldborough,* Bradford Antiquary, Vol. I, New Series, 1900.

Eboracum Lodge, Independent Order of Foresters: *Goodfellowship in Keighley, 1823-1923*, Keighley, 1925.
English, B.A., editor; *Handlist of West Riding Enclosure Awards*, National Register of Archives: West Riding (Northern Section) Committee, 1965.

Feather, W.; *History of Three Graces Lodge 408, Haworth, 1792-1931*, Keighley, 1931.
Forshaw, Charles F., editor; *The Poets of Keighley, Bingley, Haworth and District*, London, 1893.

Gale, Revd Miles; *The History of the Free School in Kighley*, *c.*1720. Typescript.
Gaskell, Mrs Elizabeth Cleghorn; *The Life of Charlotte Bronte*, London, 1857.
Gent, Thomas; *The Ancient and Modern History of the Loyal Town of Rippon*', York, 1733.
The Geological Survey of Great Britain; *Geology of the Country between Bradford and Skipton*, London, 1953.
Gomme, George Laurence, editor; *Topographical History of Worcestershire and Yorkshire: a Classified Collection of the Chief Contents of* The Gentleman's Magazine *from 1731-1868*, London, 1902.
Grierson, Edward; *A Little Farm Well Tilled', Keighley*, 1955.

Hardy, R. Spence; *Memorials of Jonas Sugden of Oakworth House*, London, 1858.
Heywood, Revd Oliver, B.A.; *Autobiography, Diaries, Anecdote and Event Books*, edited by J. Horsfall Turner. 4 volumes, Brighouse/Bingley, 1882-1885.
Hodgson, John: *Textile Manufacture, and Other Industries, in Keighley*, Keighley, 1879.
Hood, J.C.F.; *An Account of Keighley Parish Church*, Gloucester, 1935.
Hopkinson, B.; *Plans shewing the District of the Keighley Local Board of Health, Corrected and Reduced up to July, 1878*, Keighley, 1878.

Jefferys, Thomas; *The County of York*, 1771. Maps.

Keighley, William; *Keighley, Past and Present*, Keighley, 1858 and 1879.

Keighley, Borough of; *Art Gallery and Museum, Cliffe Castle: History and Collections: an Illustrated Guide*, Keighley, *c.* 1965.

Keighley, Borough of: *A Description of the Coat of Arms and Civic Regalia of the Borough of Keighley*, Keighley, 1948.

Keighley, Borough of; *The Jubilee Book of Keighley*, Keighley, 1932.

Keighley Borough of; *The Public Library Service in Keighley 1904-1954*, Keighley, 1954.

Keighley. Borough of; *Special Acts of Parliament, relating to the Borough of Keighley*, Keighley, 1895.

Keighley Local Board of Health; *Bye-Laws of the Keighley Local Board of Health: duly made and ordained by the Board, and Confirmed by Her Majesty's Principal Secretary of State for the Home Department*', Keighley, 1856 and 1864.

Keighley Parish Church National Schools, 1834-1934, Keighley, 1934.

Keighley Victoria Hospital; *Handbook*, Keighley, 1923.

Killick, H.F:, *Notes on the Early History of the Leeds and Liverpool Canal,* Bradford Antiquary, Vol. I, 'New Series, 1900.

King, J.S.; *Keighley Corporation Transport*, Huddersfield, 1964.

Laycock, John: *History of the Keighley Gas Undertaking, 1825 to 1925*, Keighley, 1925. Typescript.

Laycock, J.W.; *Methodist Heroes in the Great Haworth Round, 1734 to 1784*', Keighley, 1909.

Livett, Ronald G.C., editor; *The Parish Register of St Andrew's, Keighley*, Part III (Yorkshire Parish Register Society, 1935).

Lock, John; *A Guide to Haworth, the Brontës' Moorland Home*, Haworth, 1956.

Marchbank, W. Reid: *100 Years of Progress: an Account of the Expansion of Congregationalism in Keighley*, Keighley, 1956.

Metcalf, Thomas: *The Centenary of Wesley Chapel, Temple Street: Methodism in Keighley, 1742-1946*, Keighley, 1946.

[Milligan John]; *Baal: or, Sketches of Social Evils: a Poem, in Ten Flights*, London, 1861.

The Murrayfield Real Estate Company Ltd; *Town Centre Redevelopment, Keighley*, London, 1966.

Ogden, John, F.M.A.; *Keighley Naturalists' One Hundred Years, 1868-1968*, Keighley, 1968.

Pevsner, Nikolaus: *The Buildings of England: Yorkshire: The West Riding*, London, second edition, 1967.

Povey, R.O.T.; *The History of the Keighley and Worth Valley Railway*, Keighley, 1963.

Ranger. William: *Report to the General Board of Health on a Preliminary Inquiry into the Sewerage, Drainage; Supply of Water, and Sanitary Condition of the Inhabitants of the Town of Keighley, in the West Riding of the County of York*, London, 1855.

Recollections of the War Hospital, Keighley, and its Auxiliaries, 1916-1919, Keighley, *c.* 1920.

Rhodes, Joseph; *A Century of Keighley Baptist History, 1810-1910*, Keighley, 1910.

Rhodes, Joseph; *Half a Century of Co-operation in Keighley, 1860-1910*, Manchester, 1911.

Riley, J. Ramsden: *History of the Royal Yorkshire Lodge No. 265, Keighley, of Free and Accepted Masons of England*, Keighley, 1889.

[Rivers Commission]; *Third Report of the Commissioners Appointed to Inquire into the Best Means of Preventing the Pollution of Rivers (Rivers Aire and Calder)*: Volume I: Report, Appendix, Plans. Volume II: Minutes of Evidence and Index, London, 1867.

Schools Inquiry Commission; *Special Reports of Assistant Commissioners, and Digests of Information Received*: *Volume XVIII;* Yorkshire, London, 1869.

Scruton, William; *The Great Strike of 1825,* Bradford Antiquary, Vol. I, 1888.

Smith, A.H.; *The Place-Names of the West Riding of Yorkshire*, Part VI, English Place-Name Society, 1961..

Smith, Swire: *Educational Comparisons, or Remarks on Industrial Schools in England, Germany and Switzerland*, Keighley, 1873.

Snowden, Keighley: *The Master Spinner: a Life of Sir Swire Smith, LL.D., M.P.*', London, *c.* 1920.

Table-Moving Extraordinary: or, a Sermon and a Quantity of Poetry, given Letter by Letter, by What is Commonly Called Table-Rapping, Independent of the Will or Knowledge of the Parties Acting at the Table, Keighley, 1853.

Tate, W. E.; *The Parish Chest: a Study of the Records of Parochial Administration in England*, Cambridge, 1946.

Turner, J. Horsfall; *Haworth – Past and Present*, Brighouse, 1879.

Turner, Whiteley; *A Spring-Time Saunter round and about Brontë Land*, Halifax, 1913.

Tylecote, Mabel; *The Mechanics' Institutes of Lancashire and Yorkshire Before 1851*, Manchester, 1957.

Villy, Francis, M.D.; *The Roman Road North-Westwards from Bradford or its Neighbourhood,* Bradford Antiquary, Vol. IV, New Series, 1921.

Whitaker, Thomas Dunham; *The History and Antiquities of the Deanery of Craven*, London, 1812,

White, William; *History, Gazetteer, and Directory, of the West-Riding of Yorkshire*, Sheffield, 1837.

White, William; *Directory and Gazetteer of Leeds, Bradford, and the Whole of the Clothing Districts, of the West Riding of Yorkshire*, Sheffield, 1847 and 1853.

White, William: *Directory and Topography of the Boroughs of Leeds and Bradford*, Sheffield, 1861.

Whone, Clifford: *The Borough of Keighley: A Brief Survey of its Progress and Development during the Twentieth Century*', Keighley, *c.* 1936. Typescript.

[Wright, William] Bill o' th' Hoylus End; *Th' History o' Haworth Railway*, Keighley, 1900.

[Wright, William] Bill o' th' Hoylus End; *Poems*, Keighley, 1891.

Wing, Charles; *Evils of the Factory System, Demonstrated by Parliamentary Evidence*, London, 1837.

Yorkshire Archaeological and Topographical Association; *The Returns for the West Riding of the County of York of the Poll Tax, 1379*, London, 1882.

Newspapers and Periodicals

Keighley, Borough of: *Annual Reports of the Medical Officer of Health and the Borough Sanitary Inspector*, 1891 to date,
The Keighley and Haworth Argus, and Kildwick, Cross Hills, Steeton, and Silsden Advertiser, 1854-55.
The Keighley Herald, 1873-1911.
The *Keighley News,* 1862 to date.
The Keighley Visitor, 1853-1872.
The Keighley Year Book: A Manual of Local information and Reference, 1877-1917.
The Yorkshire Spiritual Telegraph, 1855-1856

CHAPTER ONE
Baildon: *Keighley Family*; Bawdwen: *Domesday*; Brigg: *King's Highway*: Brigg: *Keighley Parish Registers*; Cowling: *Rombalds Way*: Dickons: *Manchester to Aldborough Roman Road*; English: *Enclosure Awards*; Gale: *Free School*; Gent: *Rippon*: Gomme: *Topographical History*; Heywood: *Diaries*; Hodgson: *Textile Manufacture*; Hood: *Keighley Parish Church*; Jefferys: *County of York*; Keighley: *Keighley, Past and Present*; Killick: *Leeds and Liverpool Canal*: Livett: *Keighley Parish Register;* Smith, A.H.: *West Riding Place-Names*; Villy: *Roman Road from Bradford;* Yorkshire Archaeological and Topographical Association: *Poll Tax Returns.*

CHAPTER TWO
Ashraf: *Bradford Trades Council*; Baines: *Directory*, 1823: Briggs: *Industry and Politics*; Dewhirst: *Gleanings*; Forshaw: *Poets of Keighley*; Hodgson: *Textile Manufacture*; Keighley: *Keighley, Past and Present*; Scruton: *Strike of 1825*; Whitaker: *History of Craven*; White: *Directory*, 1837; Wing: *Evils of the Factory System.*

CHAPTER THREE
Baines: *Directory*; Barraclough: *Keighley Post Office*; Barnett: *Sladen Valley Waterworks*; Briggs: *Industry and Politics*: Dewhirst: *Gleanings*; Hodgson: *Textile Manufacture*; Keighley: *Keighley Past and Present*;:Keighley Borough: *Jubilee Book*; Laycock, J.W.: *Methodist Heroes*; Laycock, John: *Keighley Gas Undertaking;* Lock: *Guide to Haworth*; Marchbank: *100 Years;* Metcalf: *Methodism in Keighley*; Rhodes: *Keighley Baptist History*; Tate: *The Parish Chest.*

CHAPTER FOUR
Bancroft: *One Hundred Years*; Barraclough: *Keighley Post Office*; Briggs: *Industry and Politics*; Craven: *Directory*; Craven, Joseph: *Brontë Moorland Village*; Dewhirst: *Gleanings*; Eboracum Lodge: *Goodfellowship in Keighley*; Feather: *Three Graces Lodge*; Hodgson: *Textile Manufacture*; Keighley: *Keighley Past and Present*; *Keighley Parish Church National Schools*; Ranger Report: *Rhodes: 'Co-operation in Keighley*: Riley: *Royal Yorkshire Lodge*: Schools Inquiry Commission Reports; Turner: *Haworth – Past and Present*: Tylecote: *Mechanics' Institutes*: White: *Directory,* 1837 *and* 1847.

CHAPTER FIVE

Babbage Report; Brigg: *Industrial Geology of Bradford*; Dewhirst: *Gleanings*; Geological Survey: *Bradford and Skipton*; Hardy: *Memorials of Jonas Sugden*; Keighley Borough: *Special Acts of Parliament*; Keighley Local Board of Health: *Bye-Laws*; Laycock: *Keighley Gas Undertaking*; Ranger Report; White: *Directory*, 1847 and 1853.

CHAPTER SIX

Babbage Report; Barnett: *Sladen Valley Waterworks*; Caldwell: *Keighley Newspapers and Periodicals*; Dewhirst: *Gleanings*; Dewhirst: *Haworth Water-Wolf*; Forshaw: *Poets of Keighley*; Keighley: *Keighley, Past and Present*; Keighley Local Board of Health: *Bye-Laws*; Keighley Borough: *Jubilee Book*; Laycock: *Keighley Gas Undertaking*; Milligan: *Baal*; Marchbank: *100 Years*; Povey: *Worth Valley Railway*; Ranger Report; Rhodes: *Co-operation in Keighley*; Rivers Commission Report; *Table-Moving Extraordinary*; White: *Directory*, 1861; Wright: *History o' Haworth Railway*; Gaskell: *Charlotte Brontë*.

CHAPTER SEVEN

Bradford Illustrated Weekly Telegraph: *Castles and Country Houses*; Brigg: *East Riddlesden Hall*; Butterfield: *My West Riding Experiences*; Craven: *Directory*; Dewhirst: *Gleanings*; Hopkinson *Plans of the Keighley Local Board of Health*; Keighley: *Keighley, Past and Present*; Keighley Borough: *Cliffe Castle*; Keighley Borough: *Jubilee Book*; Pevsner: *Buildings of England: Yorkshire: West Riding*; Schools Inquiry Commission Reports; Smith, Swire: *Educational Comparisons*; Snowden: *Master Spinner*; White: *Directory*, 1861; Keighley Victoria Hospital: *Handbook*.

CHAPTER EIGHT

Carrodus: *J.T. Carrodus, Violinist*; Craven, C.W.: *Victoria Park*; Craven: *Directory*; Dewhirst: *Gleanings*; Dewhirst: *Haworth Water-Wolf*; Keighley: *Keighley, Past and Present*; Keighley Borough: *Public Library Service*; Keighley Borough: *Coat of Arms*; Keighley Borough: *Jubilee Book*; King: *Keighley Corporation Transport*; Ogden: *Keighley Naturalists' One Hundred Years*; Snowden: *Master Spinner*; Turner, Whiteley: *Spring-Time Saunter*; Wright: *Poems*.

CHAPTER NINE

Almond: *James Ickringill*; Dewhirst: *Haworth Water-Wolf*; King: *Keighley Corporation Transport*; *Recollections of the War Hospital*.

CHAPTER TEN

Barnett: *Sladen Valley Waterworks*; Burrow: *Keighley*; Briggs Bros: *Riddlesden*; Grierson: *A Little Farm Well Tilled*; Keighley Borough: *Jubilee Book*; King: *Keighley Corporation Transport*; Whone: *Borough of Keighley*.

CHAPTER ELEVEN

Clevely: *It Should Never Have Happened*; Murrayfleld Real Estate Company: *Town Centre Redevelopment*.

INDEX

Index

Index